All About Louisiana Birds

by Fred J. Alsop III

SWEET WATER PRESS

Birmingham, Alabama

Alsop, Fred.
All about Louisiana birds/by Fred J. Alsop III.
p.   cm.
Includes bibliographical references and index.
ISBN 1-58173-208-2
1. Birds—Louisiana. 2. Bird attracting—Louisiana I. Title.
QL684.L8A58   1997
598'.09763—dc21   97–31444
                                             CIP

10   9   8   7   6   5   4   3   2

Table of Contents

Dedication IV
Preface..V
All About Louisiana Birds 1
Attracting Birds to Your Backyard 5
    Creating the Ultimate Backyard for Birdwatching 8
    Feeders 11
    Foods 19
    Nesting Sites...29
    Plantings...40
    Dust Baths 49
    Water Sources 50
    Just for Hummingbirds..53
    Other Backyard Wildlife..59
Photographing Birds..69
    Cameras..69
    Lenses 70
    Flash Photography 71
    Film Choices 72
    Tripods 73
    Blinds 73
    Props and Backgrounds...74
Identifying Birds...77
    What to Look for on a Bird..78
    Which Is It?...80
Helpful Resource Materials...195
Index...197
About the Author..199
Birdwatching Checklist 200

To the two women in my life—

Cathi Jo,

my wife,
for all the birding trips we've taken together,
for running the wildbird feeding store,
and for loving a birder;

and in memory of

Billie Johnston Alsop,

my mother,
who loved her yard, her flowers,
and feeding the birds.

Ron Austing

Preface

The first time I remember seeing anyone feed birds was one winter morning at my grandfather's house in Kentucky when I was four or five years old. When I walked into the kitchen, I saw my grandfather standing at one of the windows looking outside at the snow-covered lawn. He was watching birds eating the cracked corn he had placed on a patch of grass he had swept clean of snow. He pointed out "red birds" (Northern Cardinals), "snowbirds" (Dark-eyed Juncos), doves, jays, and sparrows (he did not distinguish between species of sparrows; any small brown bird not a wren was a sparrow). Fascinated, I stood and watched with him for many minutes that morning. I had never really noticed birds much before, and it had never occurred to me that anyone would feed them. And though we lived on a small farm with cows, pigs, mules, chickens, dogs, and cats, I had never seen my grandfather feed a wild animal before or take pleasure in watching them.

Although I hunted, fished, and spent countless hours roaming outdoors during my boyhood days, I was not particularly interested in birds. It was not until my junior year in college that they became important to me, and ever since then the study, identification, and pleasure of watching them has been both my vocation as an ornithologist and my avocation as a birder. My interest in birds has benefited me beyond measure. It has carried me to many extraordinary places in the world, where I have seen thousands of species of birds and countless other wonders I never dreamed of in my ol' Kentucky home.

For many years I have fed birds in my backyard. I have enjoyed trying various types of seed, making suet cakes, feeding hummingbirds, building feeders and nesting boxes, trying to outwit squirrels, and planting trees, shrubs, and flowers—in short, becoming involved in all the things you do when you begin to feed birds. I have studied birds, identified birds, photographed birds, and written about them. I remain as fascinated with these colorful, delightful creatures as I was that morning fifty years ago when I took my first innocent look out my grandfather's kitchen window.

I hope that some of the experience I have gained will help you attract birds to your backyard. It doesn't matter if you plan to put out a single feeder to watch for minutes a day or you are planning a multiyear project to turn your backyard into a world-class naturescape. We already share a common bond—our love of nature.

May all the woodland creatures you desire to attract become your daily companions in your backyard. Enjoy!

Fred J. Alsop III, Ph.D.
Johnson City, Tennessee
August 1997

All About Louisiana Birds

Where you live in Louisiana will determine the birds you are most likely to see in your backyard. If you offer suitable shelter, readily available sources of water, and favorite foods, you will attract the widest variety of birds that live in or visit your region (see Attracting Birds to Your Backyard, page 5).

Keep in mind that birds are opportunists and will travel great distances through a variety of habitats to obtain whatever they need to survive. They do not understand that they have "ranges" or are expected to stay in particular regions—so you may see any bird at any time in any place. Also remember that most species have adapted to many types of habitat so Blue Jays may be just as at home in a pine forest as a mixed-hardwood forest, while Mourning Doves can be content in wetlands as well as farmlands. Ruby-throated Hummingbirds epitomize adaptability—they can be found throughout the state in all habitats. If you put up a nectar feeder, they will probably come (see Just for Hummingbirds, page 53).

If you live in a grassland or farmland area, you may have Eastern Bluebirds, Eastern Meadowlarks, Mourning Doves, Northern Bobwhites, Red-winged Blackbirds, and Common Nighthawks come to your feeders and perhaps nest on your property. During winter months you may have American

Physiographic Regions
1. Upper West Gulf Coast Plain
2. Piney Woods
3. Gulf Coast Prairies and Marshes
4. Mississippi River Alluvial Plain
5. Upper East Gulf Coastal Plain
6. East Gulf Coastal Plain

Ron Austing

Goldfinches, White-crowned Sparrows, and White-throated Sparrows at your feeders, and you may see American Kestrels hunting mice and other small ground-dwelling mammals.

If you live near a mixed-hardwood forest, keep a sharp eye out for Sharp-shinned Hawks, Cooper's Hawks, Eastern Screech-Owls, and Pileated Woodpeckers. If you live near wooded areas or parks, you will probably see Carolina Chickadees, Tufted Titmice, Blue-gray Gnatcatchers, Great Crested Flycatchers, and many other common woodland species, including nuthatches and warblers.

Hedgerows, shrubs, and overgrown fields around your home will provide shelter for Brown Thrashers, Gray Catbirds, Rufous-sided Towhees, Northern Cardinals, Indigo Buntings, and Field Sparrows. In winter months look for Dark-eyed Juncos and Carolina Wrens foraging wherever there is dense underbrush.

If you are fortunate enough to live near a mature pine forest, you will likely see Pine Warblers, Brown-headed Nuthatches, Chipping Sparrows, and in winter, Evening Grosbeaks. You may also see Cedar Waxwings foraging in pine forests and extracting seeds from pinecones.

If you live near a wetland area, you will probably see Red-winged Blackbirds, Purple Martins, Tree Swallows, Fish Crows, and Boat-tailed Grackles. Birds are instinctively attracted to water, and just providing a birdbath will bring a wide variety of birds to your backyard, including some that won't come to feeders.

Don't limit your birdwatching to your backyard—visit other regions of the state to see species you won't normally find in your neighborhood. Louisiana is as rich in bird life as it is in history. Its diverse habitats support more than 400 bird species. With nearly 7,000 miles of shoreline and about 3,500 square miles of inland water, Louisiana attracts a wide variety of waterfowl, and its proximity to the Mississippi Valley flyway makes it a favorite stopover for migrating birds that is unmatched by most other states.

The northernmost part of Louisiana features a mix of pine and hardwood forests, with extensive bottomland hardwood forests near the Mississippi River. The Tensas River National Wildlife Refuge, located near Tallulah, offers excellent opportunities to see wintering ducks as well as numerous woodland species, including songbirds, owls, and hawks. You may also see Bald Eagles here. For more information call the refuge at 318/574-2664.

The D'Arbonne National Wildlife Refuge, north of Monroe, nestles into a floodplain. Here you can see Red-shouldered Hawks, warblers, and a host of other woodland and water species. For more information write to D'Arbonne National Wildlife Refuge, 201 Jackson Street, Monroe, LA 71201.

Catahoula National Wildlife Refuge, near Walters to the south, is a migratory hotspot. This 5,000-acre birder's paradise attracts thousands of ducks and other waterfowl. For more information call 318/992-5261.

Sabine National Wildlife Refuge, near Hackberry in the prairie marshes of southwest Louisiana, provides shelter for a long list of migratory ducks, geese, pelicans, gulls, and other waterfowl. For more information call 318/762-3816.

Lacassine National Wildlife Refuge, east of Sabine, is not easily accessible but it's worth the effort to see the huge number of waterfowl that winter there. Birders have recorded sighting at least 229 species at Lacassine, including Least Terns and Peregrine Falcons. For more information call 318/774-5923.

The delta marsh region in southeast Louisiana consists of bayous, shallow Mississippi River tributaries, and ponds. The rich soil and abundant vegetation of this area attract so many species that it seems to teem with birds.

Just south of Venice you will find Delta National Wildlife Refuge, winter home to tens of thousands of ducks and geese. The relatively low human population in this area means less stress for the wildlife, making this ground sacred for both birds and birdwatchers. The delta region is an indicator of the well-being of our bird populations, which makes it essential to maintain the environmental integrity of this area. For more information call 504/646-7554.

Bogue Chitto National Wildlife Refuge sits near Bush in the bottomlands along the Bogue Chitto and Pearl Rivers. Birders

Ron Austing

have recorded sighting more than 150 species on the refuge's 26,000 acres of mixed hardwood and flooded cypress brakes. The most plentiful species seen here include turkeys, vultures, owls, and songbirds, including the elusive Swainson's Warbler. For more information call 504/863-0540.

For more information on birdwatching in Louisiana, call the Nature Conservancy at 504/338-1040 or the Audubon Institute in New Orleans at 504/861-5114.

Ron Austing

Attracting Birds to Your Backyard

Many people attract birds to their backyard as a way of getting back in touch with nature, getting back to a time when people lived as an integral part of the natural world. Other people attract birds to help reverse the current decrease in songbird populations, especially the neotropical migratory species that breed in North America but winter south of the United States in the New World tropics (neotropics). Urbanization continues to destroy natural wildlife habitats, and even the relatively small efforts we make to provide foraging areas and breeding sites in our backyards can make a tremendous difference in the survival of these birds. Also singing birds make most people feel better than traffic, sirens, machinery, and other manmade background sounds.

Still other people attract birds to upgrade their property. National Wildlife Federation studies show that landscaping

Ron Austing

increases property values as much as twenty percent and that landscaping to attract wildlife adds as much value as commercial landscaping plus the bonus of letting you watch birds and other animals in your backyard. Plantings that provide protective shading, wind screening, and humidity also reduce your home heating and cooling bills, make your home blend in better with its natural surroundings, and give you and your wildlife guests a greater degree of privacy. Providing for and watching birds and other wildlife will give you a tremendous amount of aesthetic pleasure, a quality hands-on natural history and ecology experience, and a way of relieving the stress of modern life.

Attracting birds to your backyard will let you enjoy their speedy action, great feather colors, interesting songs, and fascinating habits up close and personal. You will be able to observe the rushed stopovers of spring and fall migrant birds, the more leisurely stays of breeding birds and their fledglings, and the seasonal visits of wintering birds. You will have a front-row seat to nonstop action: the fierce diving dogfights of hummers (hummingbirds) around your nectar feeders between visits to the flowers in your yard. The constant comings and goings of chickadees and titmice as they pick out one sunflower seed at a time and fly off to a perch to peck away the seed coat. Courting male doves inflating their chests and necks and aggressively pursuing the look-alike females on the ground beneath your feeders. White-breasted Nuthatches spreading their wings and tails while pivoting in short semicircles over your suet feeder to stand off woodpeckers. The constant fluttering of activity as birds jockey for position at your feeder as well as long periods when no bird moves, as they freeze in place like feathered statues and rivet their eyes on an encroaching hawk. The shrill alarm note of a Blue Jay that sends the entire company madly dashing for the nearest cover before a predator gets close enough to launch its attack. Adults and fledglings drinking and splashing in your birdbath.

The term "backyard" does not limit you to the backyard of your house by any means. Make plans to attract birds to your backyard, side yards, and front yard as well as the land around your property. If you can talk your neighbors into sharing your interest in attracting birds, you will be able to offer a wider variety of planned habitats and thereby increase the number and variety of birds you attract. If you live in a subdivision or discrete residential area you might see if you can organize the entire neighborhood into "wildlifescaping." You may even want to hang a feeder or mount a nesting box or ledge at your workplace (see Feeders, page 11, and Nesting Sites, page 29).

If you provide suitable food, shelter, and water, birds will come to your backyard—and if you offer a wide variety of these basic necessities, you will attract a wide variety of birds. You can provide food and shelter by planting and maintaining trees, shrubs, flowers, and other vegetation (see Plantings, page 40, and Just for Hummingbirds, page 53). You can supplement the fruit, seeds, nectar, sap, and insects provided by the plants by offering feeders filled with seeds, suet, or nectar (see Feeders, page11; Food, page 19; and Just for Hummingbirds, page 53). You can supplement the available natural shelter by providing nesting boxes (see Nesting Sites, page 29) and making brush piles and other suitable "covers" (see Brush Piles, Stumps, and Snags, page 46). Nearby streams, pools, ponds, and lakes, as well as birdbaths and other sources of water (see Water Sources, page 50) will attract some species that, because of their insect or fruit diets, may not be tempted to visit your feeders. For instance, robins, bluebirds, waxwings, and a host of warblers and vireos frequent good water holes but rarely come to feeders.

Place your feeders, nesting boxes, and birdbaths where the birds will feel safe from people as well as squirrels, cats, and other animals (see Other Backyard Wildlife, page 59)—and where you can readily see the birds as you go about your daily routine. You may want to place at least one feeder a few inches from your favorite viewing window. You can buy feeders that have a one-way mirror at the back and either attach directly to the window or fit into the window like an air-conditioning unit; the birds feed in a box almost inside your home! You may find yourself spending big chunks of your day learning about the birds you see right outside your windowpane.

You are probably already interested in birds and feeding them—or you wouldn't be reading this book. If you are one of the more than sixty million Americans already hooked on making your backyard better for both you and birds, the information in the pages that follow should help you improve on the good thing you already have going.

If you haven't fed your first bird yet, just get a package of black oil sunflower seeds at your supermarket, garden center, or backyard bird feeding store, and scatter the seeds on the ground. It's that easy—you've taken your first step in attracting birds to your backyard. You can stop here or you can naturescape your entire property to attract birds and other wildlife by adding appropriate plantings (including brush piles, stumps, and snags), birdbaths and cascading waterfalls, feeders of all varieties, and hundreds of nesting boxes and shelves. You might even mount outdoor microphones connected to indoor speakers to bring the sounds of your backyard birds right inside your house.

No matter whether you stick with throwing seed on the ground or go on to create the ultimate backyard for birdwatching, perhaps the best reward of all is watching a wild creature accept your offering of food, shelter, or water. So use the following suggestions for adding feeders, food, nesting sites, plantings, dust baths, and water sources to attract birds—then pick up your binoculars and enjoy watching.

Creating the Ultimate Backyard for Birdwatching

Turning your backyard into a sanctuary for birds and other wildlife will be one of the most rewarding experiences of your life. You can make this project as simple or involved as you want, and you can do a little bit at a time or undertake major ecological "grassroots" changes all at once. Whatever changes you make will bring you hours of pleasure as you watch birds and other wild creatures come and go on a daily basis and learn firsthand about their interesting behaviors.

Getting started is as easy as hanging your first feeder, setting up a birdbath, or mounting a nesting box. You can readily buy these items, but you may want to spend an afternoon or evening building them yourself.

You may find that taking this first step and continuing to provide food, water, and shelter satisfies your desire to attract and watch birds in your backyard. Or this may be just the beginning of a project that will continue for years and include finding out about different kinds of plants and planting the trees, shrubs, and flowers that will attract the widest variety of birds to your backyard. Don't be impatient—taking your time in creating your ultimate backyard will alert you to new possibilities and also spread out the pleasure of learning more about the natural world around you.

After you have placed a feeder, birdbath, or nesting box close enough to a window so you can watch the birds up close on a daily basis, take an inventory of the elements in your backyard that already attract birds. Make a list of the established plants and what "food" they provide (nuts, berries, nectar, seeds, and fruit). Also list the kinds of insects you see in your backyard (grasshoppers, earthworms, moths, caterpillars, and others). Note natural places in your backyard that provide shelter for birds (dense shrubs, hedges, conifers, brush piles, hollow trees, rock walls, and others). Also note all the seasonal or permanent sources of water (a birdbath that can be heated in winter, and nearby springs, ponds, and streams).

Next make a sketch of your existing backyard and the surrounding natural and manmade areas, including buildings, walkways and driveways, fences, water sources, trees, gardens, and other plantings. Notice what kinds of birds frequent the natural areas outside your backyard and think about ways you can "connect" these areas to your property by planting trees and shrubs to form sheltered "traveling" corridors and safety "islands." Your goal is to provide natural dense covering, both at ground level and above, so birds and other animals can easily and safely reach your backyard sanctuary.

After you have completed your sketch, think about what ecological changes you want to make to attract the widest variety of birds to your backyard. Keep in mind both what the birds need (food, water, and shelter) and what you and the other people living in the area need (formal or informal walkways to reach different parts of the yard, etc.). Unless you are starting from scratch with only a house on a flat lawn, you already have some of the habitat diversity needed to attract a small parade of birds. Before you clear out underbrush or fencerows, burn brush piles, or cut down hollow trees, decide from the birds' point of view whether or not these natural areas meet any of their basic needs.

Before you carry out your plans, you should decide the primary purpose of your sanctuary. Do you want to attract mostly birds, and if so do you want to create a haven for them year-round or just during the winter season? Or do you want to create the ultimate backyard for all kinds of wildlife— birds, squirrels, chipmunks, bats, insects, lizards, butterflies, rabbits, frogs and toads, raccoons, and more? Knowing your primary purpose will help you make the best choices in creating your ultimate backyard.

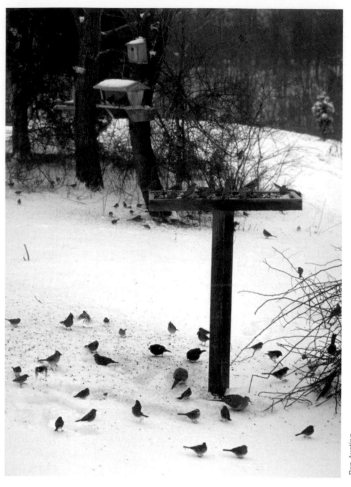

Ron Austing

The following pages will give you detailed information about feeders, food, nesting sites, plantings, dust baths, and water sources. You can find additional ideas in bird and wildlife magazines and other bird books, as well as from your county extension agent's office, your state wildlife resources agency, the Kentucky wildlife resources (to receive your Back-yard Wildlife Habitat Kit, contact Backyard Wildlife, Kentucky Department of Fish and Wildlife Resources, #1 Game Farm Road, Frankfort, KY 40601; 502/564-7863, ext. 337), and the National Wildlife Federation (for more information, write to the National Wildlife Federation, Backyard Wildlife Habitat Program, 1400 Sixteenth Street Northwest, Washington, D.C. 20036-2266).

Feeders

The greater the variety of feeders and food you provide, the greater the variety of birds that will come to your backyard. Perhaps the ultimate feeding station would have at least one of every kind of feeder available and would offer a wide variety of seeds, suet and suet mixes, and nectars.

Some feeders, such as thistle (niger) feeders for goldfinches and siskins and nectar feeders for hummingbirds, are specifically designed to attract only one or two species of birds. Others, such as platform feeders, are more generic and attract a wide range of species.

You can easily build some types of feeders using scrap wood and other materials you already have or can buy very inexpensively. If you decide to build your own feeder, check your local library for books with plans for building feeders and nesting boxes. You can also find lots of helpful information on feeders and bird-related topics on the World Wide Web.

Retailers and mail-order companies offer a wide selection of well-made, long-lasting feeders made from wood, metals, plastics, ceramics, and other materials ranging from rustic to space-age design. All of the major variety stores now have a bird-feeding section, as do building supply stores, nurseries, feed stores, farmers' co-ops, and even supermarkets. A number of national franchises specialize in backyard bird-feeding supplies. The salespeople can often tell you what food works best for each kind of feeder and the species it attracts.

The descriptions below will help you choose the feeders you need for the feeding stations in your ultimate backyard.

Platform Feeders

Platform feeders, the simplest of all feeders, take you one step up from placing the food directly on the ground. You can make a platform feeder simply by mounting a piece of plywood on a pole. If you attach a baffle between the platform and the ground, it will make it harder for climbing animals to reach the food.

Because platform feeders offer open landing areas, they attract both small and large birds, ranging from chickadees and finches to cardinals, jays, doves, rock doves (pigeons), and even woodpeckers. You can fill your platform feeders with any kind of food, and one bird or another will eagerly take almost everything you offer.

Platform feeders have several advantages. They give an open view of the birds that come to feed on it, and they are extremely easy to clean. Their big drawback is that the food is exposed to the elements. You can add a roof to help keep the food drier and free from snow, but it will cut down on your viewing area, cast a shadow that will make it harder to clearly see and photograph the birds, and perhaps discourage larger birds from trying to land on the limited exposed area.

To attract the widest variety of birds, use at least two platform feeders, one standing about a foot off the ground and the other about window height. The lower platform feeder will attract ground-feeding species, including towhees, juncos, sparrows, doves, and Northern Bobwhites, that are not comfortable at higher feeders. Almost all the other birds will come to the higher feeder, and they'll come often, making it the most popular feeder in your backyard.

Ron Austing

Hopper Feeders

Hopper feeders also attract a great variety of birds and have the added advantage of protecting the food from the weather. You can fill them with all kinds of food: small and large seeds, shelled seeds, nuts, and cracked corn. The only seed not recommended for hopper feeders is thistle—these extremely small seeds tend to attract moisture and will form lumps in feeders not especially designed for them (see Tube Feeders, page 13).

Hopper feeders provide ample landing perches for most birds, and their roofs sometimes help keep feeding birds dry.

The sides of these feeders are often made of glass or clear plastic, which lets you track the amount of food inside. A hinged or lift-up roof or a trapdoor in the roof allows quick, easy refilling.

You can easily build a hopper feeder. Traditionally they are made of wood, and some look quite rustic. They vary in size from small to gigantic. I built one for my backyard that holds more than 200 pounds of seed—plenty to feed the birds for several weeks in the winter if my wife and I leave town on an extended birding trip. To discourage squirrels from chewing on my hopper feeder and enlarging the feeding holes, I treated them with Ro-pel, a nontoxic foul-tasting chemical that penetrates wood without staining it. You can buy Ro-pel at most garden supply shops; you can also use it to stop woodpeckers from pecking at the wood part of your house and other buildings.

Tube Feeders

Tube feeders attract chickadees, titmice, finches, nuthatches, and small woodpeckers, especially Downy Woodpeckers. Tube feeders are usually made of clear plastic, which lets you easily track the amount of food inside. The best tube feeders are made of Lexan and have metal rims around the feeding holes, which makes them squirrel resistant—squirrels may still be able to reach the feeder depending on how it is mounted, but the metal generally will prevent them from enlarging the feeding holes and damaging the feeder.

Most tube feeders have short perches below the feeding holes, but some are designed for exclusive use by goldfinches and siskins and have the perch above the holes, which requires the birds to hang upside down to feed. Some of them have an attached feed tray or the option of adding an inexpensive food tray at the bottom. The small size of the perches discourages jays, doves, cardinals, and other larger birds from coming to tube feeders. If you want to attract larger birds, build or buy feeders that have a food tray, or attach one.

Tube feeders come in two distinct types: basic large-hole feeders that can dispense a variety of foods and small-hole feeders that dispense only thistle (niger) seed. Thistle feeders are designed especially for finches and will attract American Goldfinches and Pine Siskins, close "northerly" relatives of the goldfinches that occasionally invade the South for the winter. The thistle seeds that are sold commercially for these feeders do not come from the purple-flowered, sticker-laden thistle plants you see growing along roadsides—commercial thistle seeds come from a small, yellow, daisylike-flowered plant (niger) that grows in India and northeast Africa. Many people are reluctant to fill feeders with thistle seeds because they are afraid that dropped seeds will germinate and the aggressive plants will establish themselves in their backyards. Fear not—because niger is a non-native plant, the seeds are rendered inactive by heating and they will not germinate. The very small holes in thistle feeders keep the tiny black seeds from falling out and from getting wet and sticking together. You may think it would take the birds a long time to empty a feeder one tiny seed at a time, but you will be surprised at how skillfully the goldfinches manipulate these little seeds and how quickly the seed level drops. You will find yourself glued to your windowpane watching these agile birds twist themselves upside down on the perches and gobble up the seeds.

You can also attract goldfinches and siskins with inexpensive "thistle socks," open-mesh nylon bags. The birds will land on the socks and pull out the seeds from the small openings in the mesh.

You can fill large-hole tube feeders with sunflower seeds, cracked nuts, mixed seeds, or cracked corn. Since most seed mixes contain millet and other small grains preferred by ground-feeding species, I fill my tube feeders with sunflower seeds and cracked nuts, and I use the seed mixes in my platform and hopper feeders.

Many people begin with one small tube feeder filled with black oil sunflower seeds. This setup meets the basics of "feeding the birds" and provides quite a bit of enjoyment—and it makes a great gift for that difficult-to-shop-for person of any age. I suggest using a number of tube feeders and filling them with a wide variety of foods to attract the most species to your backyard.

Ball Feeders

Ball feeders are round, bowl, or satellite-shaped containers with no attached perches—only round openings at the base. They usually have an attached squirrel guard at the top.

Their design excludes all birds except those that have strong feet and are used to clinging. Chickadees, titmice, nuthatches, and woodpeckers use ball feeders with ease, and you will enjoy watching the skilled aerial acrobatics these birds perform as they perch and feed.

I suggest using only black oil sunflower seeds in ball feeders.

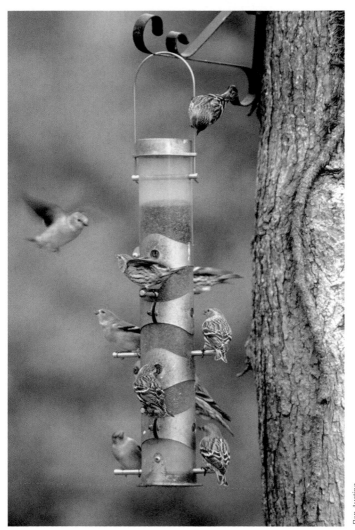

Ron Austing

Window Feeders

Window feeders let you bring birds right up to your house—
sometimes right into your house—so you can see them
close-up without using binoculars, which allows children
and housebound adults to easily enjoy these colorful, active
creatures. Window feeders work well if you live in an
apartment building or a house with limited yard space. You
may also want to mount a window feeder at your workplace
(also see Workplace Feeders, page 19).

Some window feeders attach directly to the window frame or sill, while others hang from the eaves or guttering. Some of my favorite window feeders are small, clear-plastic tubes with suction cups that attach to the windowpane. I fill one of these feeders with sunflower chips and enjoy watching the chickadees, titmice, and several finch species that regularly visit. In the summer I add a suction cup-equipped hummingbird feeder. Ruby-throated Hummingbirds come and feed so close that I can see their long tongues taking up the sugar-water nectar.

Several companies make feeders that are designed to fit into a window. All you have to do is place one of these three-sided box-style feeders into an open window with the outside of the feeder flush with the outside of your house (you fill the open space between the sides of the feeder and window frame with insulating material). The sides of the feeder, which jut into the room, are one-way mirrors that let you closely observe the birds while they feed but doesn't let them see you—or your house cat. You don't have to go outside to fill these window feeders—you add food through a port in the top from inside your room.

Nectar Feeders

Most nectar feeders are designed to attract hummingbirds and have very small feeding holes and perches. Other birds are also fond of nectar, so don't be surprised if you see orioles, mockingbirds, tanagers, chickadees, House Finches, and wood-peckers attempting to drink from your hummingbird feeder.

You can choose from a wide selection of commercial feeders ranging from small feeders that have to be filled daily to ones that hold a quart or more of nectar. Or you can make a nectar feeder from bent glass tubing, a rubber stopper, and a test-tube. You may want to add one of the new nectar feeders with larger perches and fill it with a citrus-flavored nectar mix to attract orioles or fill inexpensive poultry chick water dispensers with sugar-water nectar for larger birds.

Ants, bees, and other insects also feed on nectar. You can attach an ant moat above the feeder, fill it with water, and effectively block ants from reaching the feeder. Most nectar feeders have bee guards, barriers that prevent insects from getting close enough to suck up the nectar.

I suggest placing several nectar feeders in your backyard, spacing them apart and mounting them on or near viewing windows. You can fill the feeders with commercial ready-to-use or ready-to-mix nectar, or you can make your own nectar (see Nectar, page 26).

Hot summer sun has a greenhouse heating effect and ferments nectar in a feeder within a few days, making it unusable to the birds. Every three to four days, rinse out your feeders and add fresh nectar.

(For more about hummingbirds and nectar feeders, see Nectar, page 26, and Just for Hummingbirds, page 53.)

Fred J. Alsop III

Suet Feeders

Suet feeders are among the most interesting, effective, and inexpensive feeders. They attract woodpeckers, chickadees, titmice, nuthatches, woodpeckers, Carolina Wrens, Brown Creepers, and often wintering warblers and kinglets.

You can offer suet or suet mixes in a variety of ways, but I recommend using one of the plastic-coated wire baskets designed for them. Anchor the wire cage securely to a tree, post, or other solid object to prevent raccoons and opossums from carrying it away. (For information about commercial and homemade suet foods, see Suet and Suet Mixes, page 24.)

I keep my suet feeders filled year-round, and I especially enjoy watching adult woodpeckers bring their fledglings just out of the nest to feed. Starlings sometimes visit suet feeders, but if you want to discourage them, buy a wire basket that has a peaked roof over it so the suet can only be reached by clinging to the underside of the feeder—something starlings are loathe to do.

Fred J. Alsop III

Bluebird Feeders

Several hopper-type feeders on the market are designed to dispense currents, raisins, cornbread, fruit, berries, or commercial "bluebird mix." They lack the usual feeding holes, and birds enter the feeders from the ends through bluebird-size holes. Tufted Titmice also quickly learn to use bluebird feeders.

Personally I have had poor results attracting bluebirds to these feeders, but other people I know have been more successful. One person in my area attracts bluebirds to a platform feeder in her backyard. She feeds them a steady diet of cornbread that she makes "with as much corn oil as it will hold." I have seen as many as six Eastern Bluebirds at a time eagerly downing her crumbled cornbread in winter.

Woodpecker Feeders

Perches on tube feeders tend to exclude woodpeckers, and they have a hard time trying to find a place on hopper and platform feeders to brace their stiff tails so they can feed in an upright position. Feeders designed for woodpeckers have a support they can use to brace their tails. These feeders also have ³/₄-inch-thick walls that prevent almost all birds except woodpeckers from feeding on the nuts, corn kernels, sunflower seeds, or peanuts inside. Only woodpeckers and White-breasted Nuthatches have bills long enough to reach the food.

If you're looking for a feeder that your neighbors probably don't own, or for a feeder for a backyard birder who has everything, get a woodpecker feeder.

Workplace Feeders

You don't have to limit your enjoyment of feeding birds or watching wildlife to the time you spend at home. Even if your work keeps you indoors for most of the day, you may be able to find a spot outside the building to mount one or more feeders that you and your coworkers can enjoy. My dentist keeps several bird feeders positioned outside the large windows of his office, and I always enjoy (as I am sure his other patients do) the diversion of watching birds coming to and going from these feeders when I sit in his dentist's chair.

If you have a window in the area where you work you may be able to put up a small window ledge feeder or a nectar feeder (see Window Feeders, page 15, and Nectar Feeders, page 16). Window feeders are easy to maintain, and they attract a lot of birds. Being able to look up from your work occasionally and watch a colorful bird at your feeder is both satisfying and relaxing.

Foods

To attract the widest variety of birds to your feeding stations, offer as many foods in as many different kinds of feeders as you can. Use the information on the following pages to help you choose foods to attract the birds you especially want to watch in your ultimate backyard.

Seeds

Americans spend more than $2 billion on birdseed each year. Seeds are easy to store and dispense, they're relatively inexpensive, and birds eat them year-round. Sunflower seeds and "wild bird mixes" have been widely available for many years, and other seeds can now be found at local stores and through mail-order sources.

Striped Sunflower Seeds

Striped sunflower seeds are larger (they can be up to $1/2$ inch long) than black oil sunflower seeds (see below) and have longitudinal dark and light stripes on the seed coat. Since the hulls are too thick for most small birds to break open, striped sunflower seeds tend to pile up quickly under feeders.

Birds that like sunflower seeds: cardinals, jays, grosbeaks, chickadees, titmice, nuthatches, and woodpeckers.

Black Oil Sunflower Seeds

Black oil sunflower seeds are the generic seeds of birdfeeding—if you want to put only one kind of seed in your feeders, this is it! More bird species will eat these small, oil-rich (calorie-rich) seeds than any other kind. Be sure to offer black oil sunflower seeds in at least one of your feeders.

Black-oil sunflower seeds are easily distinguished by their small size (they are about $1/4$ inch long) and dark, almost black seed coat. Their small size makes them easy for birds to carry off, and their thinner hull makes them easier than striped sunflower seed to break open. Their smaller seed coats also mean that less waste will pile up under your feeders.

Ron Austing

Birds that like black oil sunflower seeds: all seed-eating birds, including woodpeckers.

Hulled Sunflower Seeds (Chips/Hearts)

Choose hulled sunflower seeds (also called sunflower chips or hearts) if you want to feed the birds without having to periodically rake up the seed coats that accumulate beneath your feeders. I almost always use hulled sunflower seeds in window feeders that are over patios, walks, porches, or driveways. Hulled sunflower seeds cost more per pound, but remember that you are not paying for the weight of the seed coats as you do for unhulled seeds.

Birds that like hulled sunflower seeds: all seed-eating birds, especially goldfinches, siskins, House Finches, and Carolina Chickadees.

Safflower Seeds

If you have not offered safflower seeds before, you may have to introduce these white seeds to your birds by mixing them with sunflower seeds and gradually working to straight safflower seeds. If you want to discourage squirrels and blackbirds from using your feeders, fill them with safflower seeds—neither species likes them.

Birds that like safflower seeds: doves, cardinals, House Finches, White-throated Sparrows, and Tufted Titmice.

White Proso Millet Seeds

These small, round, bone-colored seeds are often found in "wild bird" seed mixes. Ground-feeding birds relish white proso millet, and it works well in mixes used for hopper and platform feeders.

Birds that like white proso millet seeds: doves, cardinals, towhees, juncos, and all species of sparrows.

Red Millet Seeds

These small, round reddish seeds (not to be confused with the larger BB-size milo seeds) are often found in seed mixes. Birds don't like it as much as white millet.

Birds that like red millet seeds: doves and most sparrows.

Milo Seeds

Milo is one of the sorghum grains, and BB-size reddish brown milo seeds are often found in "wildbird" mixes. Seeds from mature milo grain have very hard seed coats and taste somewhat bitter. Birds that eat milo seeds tend to swallow them whole. While birds in the Midwest and southwestern United States eat great quantities of milo seeds, most Southern birds rake them out of feeders, leaving them to germinate in your backyard. I suggest buying mixes that contain little or no milo seeds.

Birds that like milo seeds: Northern Bobwhites, turkey, doves, and ducks.

Thistle (Niger) Seeds

These tiny black seeds do not come from the wild thistle plants you see growing in fields and along roadsides; they come from the niger plant (a yellow-flowering, daisylike plant that doesn't have stickers on leaves and stems) that grows in India and northeast Africa. These imported seeds are heat-treated to prevent them from germinating. Thistle seeds should be used in feeders especially designed to dispense them (for more about thistle feeders, see Tube Feeders, page 13).

Perhaps the only drawback to using thistle seeds is their price—these tiny, oil-rich seeds generally cost more per pound than other seeds. But when you consider the slow rate at which they disappear based on the huge number of them it takes to fill a feeder (there are more than 150,000 thistle seeds in a pound), you get a lot of viewing pleasure and birdfeeding for your dollar. I heartily suggest trying a thistle feeder in your backyard.

Birds that like thistle (niger) seeds: American Goldfinches, Pine Siskins, Purple Finches, House Finches, and Carolina Chickadees.

Corn

Whole kernels and shelled corn, which are available in bulk from most feed stores and farmers' co-ops, work well for platform feeders. Placing some ears of corn on the cob on the ground will help keep squirrels and raccoons away from the more expensive foods in your feeders and from interfering with feeding birds.

Birds that like corn: Northern Bobwhites, Wild Turkeys, doves, jays, grackles, blackbirds, and crows.

Cracked Corn

Birds can carry off and eat cracked corn easier than whole corn. It works well in mixes for hopper and platform feeders.

Ron Austing

I don't recommend using cracked corn in feeders in urban areas unless you want to attract lots of House Sparrows and Rock Doves (Pigeons).

Birds that like cracked corn: doves, sparrows, bobwhites, turkeys, ducks, blackbirds, and starlings.

Nuts

Peanuts

A great variety of birds will eagerly feed on peanuts and a commercial mix called "peanut pickouts." Placed in hopper, platform, and even tube feeders, either alone or in a mix, peanuts will disappear quickly. To thwart the squirrels from eating up all the peanuts, place them in a feeder made from 1/4-inch mesh hardware cloth.

Birds that like peanuts: Carolina Chickadees, Tufted Titmice, American Goldfinches, Pine Siskins, sparrows, jays, crows, and kinglets.

Unsalted Peanuts in the Shell

Bags of these unsalted peanuts in the shell are available most of the year in the Southeast, and they can be used as a substitute for suet in the summer. You can either place the peanuts on platform feeders or just throw them on the ground.

Birds that like unsalted peanuts in the shell: Tufted Titmice, jays, and woodpeckers.

Ron Austing

Nut Meats (Walnuts, Almonds, Pecans, and Others)

While nut meats may be expensive fare compared with other foods for birds, they are sometimes available at co-ops and farmers' markets in bulk. Whenever you offer them, the birds will surely enjoy them.

Birds that like nut meats: Carolina Chickadees, Tufted Titmice, nuthatches, jays, and woodpeckers.

Suet and Suet Mixes

Pure suet is nothing more than beef fat and is available at your supermarket meat counter or meat market. Raw suet attracts many birds, including woodpeckers, but it goes rancid quickly in hot summer days. I suggest using raw suet only during cooler weather.

If you want to make suet cakes, cut raw suet into $1/2$-inch chunks and cook it over low heat until the oil is rendered out. Then mix in as much cornmeal (the cheapest brand you can buy) as it will hold, along with peanut butter, raisins, and mixed seeds. Pack the suet mixture into a wax-paper milk carton or Tupperware container, and refrigerate it overnight. Cut off pieces of the "set" mixture to fit your wire baskets. The rendered fat will not spoil, even in the summer heat.

You can also buy suet cakes. You will find a bewildering array of suet mixtures at stores that sell birdseed. The cheapest high-energy cakes are as good as any other kinds, and the birds will love them all. In hot weather months, look for no-melt suet "dough" cakes—they won't melt and run right out of the holder like regular suet cakes do.

Birds that like suet and suet mixes: Woodpeckers, Carolina Chickadees, Tufted Titmice, Carolina Wrens, nuthatches, Brown Creepers, warblers, European Starlings, and some thrushes.

Fruit

You may not have considered fruit as a part of the larder you can offer to birds, but some birds prefer fruit and berries. Bluebirds, tanagers, and orioles will never frequent your seed feeders no matter how many different varieties of seeds or how many different kinds of feeders you place in your backyard. But apples will lure colorful bluebirds to a feeder, and citrus fruit may entice richly plumaged orange-and-black orioles to be regular visitors.

Apples

Slice apples in half and offer them cut side out on a nail driven into a post, feeder, or tree. Or dice apples and place them in a food dish attached to a feeder to attract Eastern Bluebirds and American Robins.

Birds that like apples: Jays, orioles, robins, bluebirds, mockingbirds, grosbeaks, and woodpeckers.

Bananas

Lots of tropical birds eat bananas and many of our summering songbirds spend their winters in the tropics, but we don't often think of or see bananas offered to birds at feeders because they spoil so quickly. You can make bananas last longer by leaving on the peel and slicing them into inch-long sections and placing them on the feeder or by removing only one longitudinal section of peel. (Also see Ripe Bananas, page 26.)

Birds that like bananas: Northern Mockingbirds, Summer Tanagers, American Robins, Northern Orioles, and warblers.

Grapes, Raisins, and Soaked Raisins

Grapes are readily taken by a number of species of birds and will go further if you slice them before placing them in your feeders. Many birds eat raisins as they are, but for variety try soaking them in water and offer the "instant" grapes at your feeders—you'll cause quite a commotion!

Birds that like grapes, raisins, and soaked raisins: Eastern Bluebirds, American Robins, Cedar Waxwings, Northern Mockingbirds, Gray Catbirds, woodpeckers, Rose-breasted Grosbeaks, European Starlings, and Carolina Wrens.

Oranges

Slice oranges in half and offer them cut side out on a nail driven into a post, feeder, or tree (loose sliced and sectioned oranges are quickly carried away). You can also fasten orange halves to a platform feeder, a plank placed on the ground, or a tree branch close to the ground.

Birds that like oranges: orioles, tanagers, mockingbirds, thrashers, and woodpeckers.

Ripe Bananas

You can hang ripe bananas near your bird feeders to attract fruit-eating birds as well as insects, including fruit flies—which in turn will attract small insectivorous birds that will enjoy the concentration of live, fast food. (Also see Bananas, page 25.)

Birds that like ripe bananas: hummingbirds (they will feed on the fruit flies), warblers, and Blue-gray Gnatcatchers.

Nectar

For most of us, attracting hummingbirds by filling feeders with sugar-water nectar is a summertime ritual, and if you live in the Deep South, you may have also used sugar-water feeders to attract wintering hummingbirds as well. In recent winters hummingbirds have been seen in almost all of the Southeastern states, and some people provide nectar year-round to attract these seasonal visitors from the West—as well as a number of other species.

Commercial ready-to-use and ready-to-mix nectars are available, but most contain red dyes that may be harmful to birds' kidneys. (Red flowers are known to attract hummingbirds, and most hummingbird feeder manufacturers add sufficient red areas to their feeders so that no red is needed in the nectar itself.)

You can easily make sugar-water nectar by adding one part sugar to four parts boiling water. Do not add red dye or honey to your homemade nectar; neither ingredient is needed to attract birds. Let the nectar cool before filling your feeders,

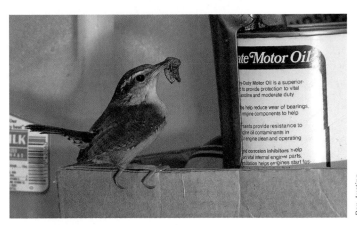

Ron Austing

and refrigerate any leftovers. (For more about nectar, see Nectar Feeders, page 16).

Birds that like nectar: hummingbirds, orioles, woodpeckers, and some finches.

Extras on the Menu

Here are some suggested foods that have been featured in magazines for birders or passed around in bird-feeding circles.

Peanut Butter

This high-energy food that lots of birds like is inexpensive (the cheapest brand suits the birds just fine), readily available, and easy to use. If you are concerned about it being too sticky for the birds to eat, mix the peanut butter with cornmeal (which the birds also like). You can experiment by adding suet, cracked corn, seeds, and raisins, and then cooking the mixture to blend the ingredients.

Spread peanut butter or your peanut butter mixture into the crevices of pine cones, cracks in a log or tree trunk, or 1/2-inch holes drilled in a limb or piece of 4 x 4 (suspend the 4 x 4 from a limb or other hanger)—and enjoy watching the birds flock to it. Peanut butter will also attract ants—which the birds may eat as well, but if you don't want to be overrun with ants, you may want to save this treat for colder weather.

Birds that like peanut butter: wrens, warblers, finches, jays, woodpeckers, thrashers, Eastern Bluebirds, Carolina Chickadees, Tufted Titmice, and nuthatches.

27

Grape Jelly

You can attract orioles by placing some inexpensive generic-brand grape jelly in small, shallow ($1/2$ to 1-inch deep, 3 to 4-inch wide) trays fastened to your bird feeders. Try this in the summer when the orioles are around—it may be just the ticket to get them down out of the treetops on a daily basis.

Birds that like grape jelly: Baltimore Orioles, Orchard Orioles, Gray Catbirds, and American Robins.

Crushed Eggshells

Birds, particularly adult females, especially like crushed eggshells in the spring and summer when they are nesting. Female birds produce the shells for the eggs they lay from calcium they obtain from the foods they eat and from their own skeletal system.

Birds that like crushed eggshells: almost all birds.

Grit

"Rare as hen's teeth" is an old cliche that points out the fact that no modern bird has teeth. Many birds, especially seed-eating species, use powerful muscles in their gizzards to help grind up their food. The gizzard, a muscular stomach-like organ, holds grit in the form of sand and small stones swallowed by birds to help in the grinding process. Grit is readily available most of the year except in those states where winter snows cover the ground for lengthy periods. Birds will appreciate having a scoop of sand on a platform feeder or in a shallow container near a feeder.

Birds that like grit: almost all seed-eating birds.

Live Food

For a special treat that many birds will relish, place a scoop of live insects on your feeding platforms or trays. Many species that won't visit your feeders for any other reason will come again and again if you offer live insects.

Offering live insects is not as difficult or expensive as you may think. You can find inexpensive mealworms at many pet shops, pet sections in some of the larger variety stores, and sometimes at bait supply stores. Or you can raise meal-worms. A starter set of 1,000 mealworms costs less than $5. Place the mealworms in a plastic container with cornmeal, oatmeal, or bran flakes topped with shredded newspaper and a slice of apple or potato. Cover the container with screen wire to keep in the insects and add a fresh slice of apple or potato once a week. Place some of the mealworms in a dish each day on the feeder, and watch how quickly they are snapped up by the birds.

If you have a bug-zapper, you have another easy source of live insects. Try suspending a steep-sided plastic tray beneath the bug-zapper to catch insects that would normally fall to the porch floor or ground. Many of the insects are not killed but will be trapped in your tray. Leave enough space between the tray and the bug-zapper for birds to fly in and retrieve the bugs. If you don't have a bug-zapper, just put an ultraviolet lightbulb in your porch light fixture and hang your collecting tray under the light.

Birds that like live insects: vireos, warblers, woodpeckers, sparrows, finches, Carolina Chickadees, Tufted Titmice, Blue-gray Gnatcatchers, Eastern Bluebirds, American Robins, wrens, nuthatches, kinglets, jays, and mimic thrushes.

Ron Austing

Nesting Sites

Providing suitable nesting habitats will attract both permanent residents and migratory breeding birds. Once again, creating this part of your ultimate backyard can be as simple or involved as you want to make it.

Much of the naturescaping you have done or plan to do will provide the necessary shelter for many bird species (see Plantings, page 40). You can also buy or build nesting boxes and platforms to meet the specific needs of birds you particularly want to watch.

Ron Austing

Woodpeckers and other primary-cavity nesters excavate their own cavities, while secondary-cavity nesters either find suitable natural cavities or abandoned woodpecker holes. The cavity nests birds make in trees or wooden posts are naturally rustic—so even if your carpentry skills are second to those of Tim on *Home Improvement,* you will probably be able to build a nesting box that at least one homeless secondary-cavity nester would welcome.

Suitable nesting cavities are often at a premium and in such demand that birds compete fiercely for them. Scientific studies have shown that the lack of nesting cavities limits the number of some bird species. When researchers supplied artificial nesting boxes over several consecutive breeding seasons, some bird populations increased significantly. Some birds have become so adapted to nesting in manmade nesting cavities that they are rarely seen in natural settings. When was the last time you saw a Purple Martin or a Chimney Swift nesting in something other than a manmade nesting box, a hollowed-out gourd, or a chimney (for swifts)?

Birds other than cavity nesters also sometimes have trouble finding suitable nesting sites and will accept help from people. Dr. Jerry Nagel, a colleague and friend of mind, became interested in the nesting success of Eastern Phoebes several summers ago. He checked under ten concrete high-way culverts in Upper East Tennessee and found three nesting pairs of Eastern Phoebes. That fall, after the phoebes had stopped all their breeding activities and the year's fledglings had left the nests, Jerry glued small wooden nesting ledges inside each of the culverts. When we checked the culverts the next year, all ten of them had nesting phoebes—and every phoebe nest was built squarely on one of Jerry's wooden ledges.

Years ago two other friends, Ron Austing and Jack Holt, built artificial nests from old automobile tires, hardware cloth, straw, and sticks and placed them 40 feet or higher in trees in scattered woodlots in the rolling hill country of southwestern Ohio. More than seventy percent of the artificial nests were used by Great Horned Owls that evidently had been unable to locate natural suitable nesting sites in the region's cut-over forests.

American Robins, Eastern Phoebes, and Barn Swallows will nest on simple wooden shelves attached to buildings or under bridges and culverts, particularly if the shelves are placed under the shelter of an overhanging eave, porch, awning, or other protective covering. If you live by a large pond, lake, river, or other body of water, you may want to build nesting platforms for area waterbirds. A 20 to 30-foot pole set in open water with a 45-inch-square platform on top will attract ospreys. Place some sticks on the platforms to get them started on building their nests, and enjoy watching these fish-eating birds of prey raise their young.

Great Blue Herons prefer platforms raised about 30 feet above the water either near or on the shore. To protect young herons from ground predators, add a metal guard around the pole about 5 feet above the water or shore. For the nesting platform, use wooden slats to build an open 30-inch-long triangular structure. Make one side of the triangle 84 inches long—the extra 4 feet will serve as a perch; rounding the slats of the perch will make it easier for the birds to stand on it.

Canada Geese prefer "island" nesting sites. You can create artificial islands by placing 48-inch-square platforms on log or rigid-foam rafts. Attach either a metal washtub or an old tire to the top of the wooden platforms, and then anchor the rafts well out in the water to protect the nesting adults, eggs, and fledglings from ground predators.

If you are not handy with tools or don't have the time, materials, or equipment to build nesting boxes or platforms, you can find a wide variety of ready-made and precut nesting materials at hardware, variety, and bird-feeding stores.

Use the information on the following pages to help you provide a variety of nesting sites at both your house and workplace. Being a landlord for the birds doesn't take much time or effort, and the excitement of watching birds court their mates and raise their families will provide hours of pleasure.

Building Nesting Boxes, Platforms, and Ledges

The Tennessee Wildlife Resources Agency offers a free forty-page booklet called *Woodworking for Wildlife in Tennessee.* This booklet gives helpful drawings and instructions for building a variety of nesting boxes and platforms that can be made by anyone who has basic carpentry skills. The nesting structures shown in the booklets can be used in backyards across the Southeastern United States. To get your free copy, write to Tennessee Wildlife Resources Agency, Ellington Agricultural Center, P.O. Box 40407, Nashville, TN 37204.

To make sure that the nesting sites you build have the best chance of attracting birds and providing safe shelter for them for at least ten years, keep the following tips in mind.

- Build each box or platform for a specific kind of bird rather than just building for the "birds." Different species have different house-size and entrance-hole requirements, and birds will be attracted to nesting sites that are just right for them (see Providing Nesting Sites for the Birds You Want to Attract, page 38).

- Nesting boxes must have a hinged side, front, or roof so they can be easily checked and cleaned out after each brood of fledglings has left and at the end of the breeding season. Be sure to use rust-proof hinges when you make nesting boxes.

- Use locking clips (like those on dog leashes) instead of hooks and eyes to secure the hinged opening on Wood Duck and owl boxes to prevent raccoons from opening them. If you can't find locking clips, add a row of large-head roofing nails on the side of the roof and a matching row on the upper edge of the box sides; run wire around the "pairs" of nails to hold the hinged opening tightly shut.

- Extend the roof of the nesting box at least 2 inches beyond the front to help prevent water from getting inside during heavy rainstorms. (Mounting nesting boxes with the entrance holes facing away from prevailing winds will also help keep out rainwater.) Drill at least 1 ($1/4$-inch) drain hole in each corner of the floor. Drill several ($1/4$-inch) holes or cut several slots near the top of the box to allow warm air to escape on hot summer days.

- Almost every carpenter thinks that a "proper" birdhouse has to have a perch below the entrance hole, but avoid the temptation. North American cavity-nesting birds have

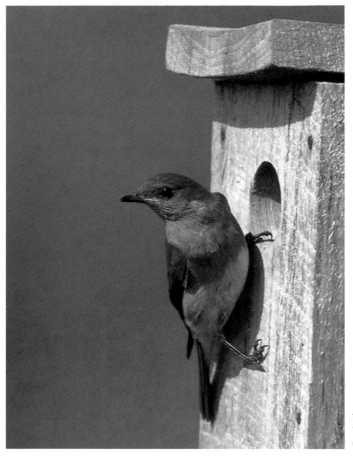

Ron Austing

strong grasping feet and don't need perches. House
Sparrows and European Starlings don't need perches, but
perches make it easier for them to successfully prevent
other birds from using the nesting boxes. Bluebirds, Tree
Swallows, and other native species can often displace
House Sparrows and European Starlings when these non-
native "undesirables" don't have the advantage of a perch.
So if you buy or already have nesting boxes that have
perches, take them off. The only time you might want to
attach a "perch" is when you build a Wood Duck nesting
box. Fastening a slab of wood, with the bark still on it,
horizontally under the entrance hole of Wood Duck
nesting boxes makes it easier for these birds to land at
the opening, although they, too, will do fine without
a perch.

Ron Austing

- Use ³/₄-inch-thick wood when you make nesting boxes to insulate the interior from the cold snaps of late spring and the heat of Southern summers. Pine works well for smaller boxes, but use cedar, redwood, or cypress for most larger ones. You can use pine or plywood for Wood Duck, owl, flicker, and martin nesting boxes if you treat the outside surfaces of the boxes with earthtone paints, stains, or preservatives (you can use white paint for martins only). If you plan to mount a nesting box on a post or tree, put several coats of paint, stain, or preservative on the back side to help keep it from rotting. Do not paint or otherwise treat the inside of nesting boxes.

    Do not use wood treated with green copper-based preservative because it can produce poisonous vapors when it is exposed to water, and do not paint, stain or treat a wooden nesting box with creosote.

- *Do not* make nesting boxes from tin cans or other metal materials, or from milk cartons. Metals heat up like ovens in direct sun and the heat will "cook" the eggs and nestlings. Milk cartons provide little insulation and temperatures inside range widely, often lethally.

    Commercial Purple Martin houses made from lightweight, airplane-grade aluminum and artificial gourd houses for martins, wrens, and other birds have been well field-tested for keeping inside temperatures in a healthy range. Commercial plastic Wood Duck houses have also been tested and approved, but be sure to place them in shady locations.

● Use galvanized nails or screws because they don't rust. Screws work better than nails because they accommodate the expansion, contraction, and warping of wood as it heats, cools, and weathers. Use concrete-coated or ring shank nails to prevent the sides, roof, and floorboards from loosening.

● Nail the sides of the nesting box to the edges (rather than the top) of the floorboard to keep rainwater from seeping into the crack between the sides and the floor and then up into the nest. Recess the floorboard about 1/4 inch up from the bottom of the sides to help prevent moisture from seeping across the underside of the floor and up the sides.

● You can suspend small nesting boxes for wrens under the eaves of your house or from a tree limb, but all other nesting boxes should be firmly attached to a post, tree, or building. Use lag screws and washers when you attach nesting boxes to living trees so you can gradually unscrew them to allow for the tree's growth—otherwise the tree will slowly pull the screws through the wood and damage the house.

● Mount bluebird nesting boxes on posts out in the open. Do not mount bluebird boxes on trees because bluebirds don't like overhanging branches and the many birds that do prefer houses on trees will compete strongly for them.

● Space nesting boxes far apart to reduce competition and territorial conflicts. A good rule-of-thumb is to allow about an acre of habitat for birds of the same species, but there are some exceptions. Bluebird boxes should be placed at least 100 yards apart, but you can mount two of them back-to-back and often have the second box occupied by the pair that just finished their first nesting of the season in the first box. Since Purple Martins and Wood Ducks tolerate other birds from their species, place martin boxes in "apartment style" colonies and place gourds in clusters. You can group Wood Duck boxes in clusters of two, three, or four.

● Small animals may take up residence in your bird nesting boxes—after all they don't know the boxes were intended for other tenants. If you don't want resident mice, squirrels, flying squirrels, opossums, and raccoons or visiting snakes (usually just looking for dinner), you will have to evict them. On the other hand, if you are creating an ultimate backyard for the benefit of all wildlife, you may decide just to provide enough boxes to accommodate the birds as well as unexpected creatures.

- In early spring check your nesting boxes for mice nests, and evict the mice before the birds start looking for nesting sites. Some people advise just leaving the "door" of the nesting box open during the winter to discourage mice, but many birds, including bluebirds, use the boxes as nightly roosts, especially during cold winter weather when a whole family of birds may snuggle inside for protection and shared body heat.

- To evict wasps and bees, spray the insects and their nests with insecticide and remove the nests after the adults are dead. Then spray the interior of the box with Lysol or another disinfectant.

- To evict ants, spray the colony with Terro or another commercial ant killer or spray some of the ant killer into a bottle cap and place it under the nesting box.

- Blowfly eggs and larvae will sometimes become established in a bluebird nest, and the larvae will suck blood from the young birds, weakening them and sometimes causing death. If you see blowflies, gently lift up the bluebird nest and lightly tap it with your fingers. The larvae will fall through the nesting material to the floorboard, and then you can brush them out of the box.

- House Sparrows and European Starlings are non-native bird species brought to the United States from Europe, and they are not protected by our state or federal laws. So if you really don't want them in your nesting boxes, you can legally remove them—nests, eggs, and fledglings. These birds are often persistent, and you may have to evict them five or six times before they give up and abandon your nesting box. You can trap adult birds on their nests at night by placing a plastic bag over the entrance hole and opening the box or tapping on it sharply to drive them into the bag. Double check the descriptions for House Sparrows (see page 193) and European Starlings (see page 149) to positively identify the birds occupying your nesting box so you don't toss out or discourage "desirable" species that are protected by law.

  I don't advocate killing any animal though, and personally I find House Sparrows and European Starlings

Ron Austing

just as fascinating as our native birds. Instead of killing these birds, I suggest discouraging them from nesting by providing nesting boxes designed specifically for other species (see Providing Nesting Sites for the Birds You Want to Attract, page 38).

● Any nesting box with an entrance hole at least 1 3/8 inches or larger will admit House Sparrows, and an entrance hole 1 1/2 inches or larger will admit European Starlings. To prevent these "undesirable" species, don't make entrance holes any larger than needed to fit the species you want to attract.

● Place wood chips rather then sawdust in your nesting boxes for birds that prefer woody materials as a base for their nests and for birds that don't deposit their eggs directly on the floorboard. Sawdust is small with lots of surface area, and it tends to pack down and hold moisture when it gets wet. Wood chips retain less water and provide better drainage for the nest.

Owls, American Kestrels, Wood Ducks, and Hooded Mergansers like to have a layer of wood chips on the floor of their nesting boxes. Woodpeckers and nuthatches prefer that you overfill their nesting boxes with wood chips so they can toss out a lot of them and at least partially satisfy their instinct to "dig" a cavity.

● You do not need to equip your nesting boxes with "escape ladders" for most bird species, with the possible exception of Tree Swallows. Adults caught by early spring cold snaps often take refuge in nesting boxes, and sometimes an escape ladder—a piece of hardware cloth fastened inside the box from just beneath the entrance hole to the floorboard—may make the difference of whether or not a weakened adult can get back up to the hole and leave the box when the weather improves.

● Always mount a metal cone as a predator guard on any wooden post or tree used to hold a nesting box or platform.

Providing Nesting Sites for the Birds You Want to Attract

The table on the next page lists the nesting box requirements of some of the species you may want to attract to nesting boxes in your backyard. I did not include House Sparrows or European Starlings because they will come whether or not you build specifically for them. Most woodpeckers prefer to excavate their own nesting cavities, and I listed only those species that will accept a nesting box on a somewhat regular basis.

In general, drill the entrance hole 1 or 2 inches from the top on the front side of each nesting box. For Purple Martins, drill the entrance hole 1 inch from the floor.

Woodworking for Wildlife in Tennessee, the free booklet offered by the Tennessee Wildlife Resources Agency (see page 32), includes building plans for all of the nesting boxes listed on page 39.

Ron Austing

Nesting Boxes

Species	Size of Box Height (in.)	Floor (in.)	Entrance Hole Diameter (in.)	Height above Ground (ft.)	Remarks
American Kestrel	14-16	9 x 9	3	12-30	on tree/post in open country
Eastern Screech-Owl	15-18	8 x 8	3	10-30	on tree/post/building in wooded area
Northern Flicker	16-18	7 x 7	2½	8-20	on tree in wooded area
Red-headed Woodpecker	12-16	6 x 6	2	12-20	on tree in wooded area
Red-bellied Woodpecker	12-16	6 x 6	2½	12-20	on tree in wooded area
Great Crested Flycatcher	10-12	6 x 6	2	8-20	on tree/post in wooded area
Purple Martin	6	6 x 6	2¼	8-20	on post in open area; best near water
Tree Swallow	6-8	5 x 5	1½	5-15	on post in open area; best near water
Tufted Titmouse	8-10	4 x 4	1⅛	5-15	on tree/post in wooded area
Carolina Chickadee	8-10	4 x 4	1⅛	5-15	on tree/post in wooded area
Nuthatches (all species)	8-10	4 x 4	1¼	10-20	on tree in wooded area
Carolina Wren	6-8	4 x 4	1½	5-10	on tree/post/building in wooded area
House Wren	6-8	4 x 4	1⅛	5-10	on tree/post/building near people
Eastern Bluebird	8	5 x 5	1½	5-10	on post in open area/meadow
House Finch (occasional user)	6	6 x 6	1½	6-12	on tree/post/building near people

Plantings

Think of planting trees, shrubs, and other vegetation as an investment. They add to the resale value of your property, make your home more energy-efficient, improve the appearance of your property, cut down on the amount of grass you have to mow—and they also provide food and cover for birds and other wildlife. When you consider all the benefits, you can readily justify the cost of naturescaping.

When you are planning your ultimate backyard, include a diversity of plants that will attract a wide variety of birds. Decide what species you especially want to see, and then use the information in this book (see descriptions of birds commonly seen in the Southeast, starting on page 91) and other books (see Helpful Resource Materials, page 195) to determine what plants meet the food and shelter needs of those species.

As you decide what existing plants to keep on your property and what new ones to add, remember that your backyard must meet your needs as well as the birds. Also keep in mind that the larger the area you naturescape, the greater the diversity and number of birds you can attract.

You may want to invite your neighbors to join you in creating wildlife corridors and continuous strips of natural areas that cross property lines. Working together to naturescape an entire neighborhood will not only provide a wider diversity of natural food and shelter, but it will also increase the value of everyone's property. Whether or not your neighbors take an active role in your naturescaping project, be sure the changes you make to your property don't adversely affect their property.

Evaluating Your Existing Naturescape

The first step in naturescaping is to evaluate what you already have on your property.

STEP 1: Draw a "map" that shows your property lines, existing buildings, fences, walkways, driveways, areas of trees/shrubbery/lawn, and streams/ponds/other natural sources of water. Also sketch in above and below ground wiring, water pipes, septic tanks and drain fields, sewer lines, gas lines, and any other features you know about.

Being aware of what's already on your property will help you plan where to fit in "new" plantings so roots don't grow into drain tiles and trees don't reach up into wiring. It will also let you know areas to avoid so you don't inadvertently cut into underground wiring with a shovel or break a water pipe with a backhoe.

Ron Austing

STEP 2: Notice what areas of your property get sun at different times of the day and during different seasons. Indicate these areas on a piece of clear plastic that you can place over your property "map." Also indicate on the plastic overlay any low-lying areas that tend to stay moist.

Examine the soil in various areas on your property and note on the plastic overlay where you have top soil, clay, sand, sandy loam, fill dirt, or some combination. Buy a soil test kit at a garden supply or variety store and check the soil pH of the different areas.

The amount of sunlight and moisture, the type of soil, and the pH of the soil will determine what plants will grow best in each area of your property.

STEP 3: Make a list of the trees, shrubs, vines, and other plants already growing on your property. Note their size, age, health, whether they are native to your state, their energy conservation value (do they lower cooling/heating costs by shading your home in summer or acting as windbreaks in the winter?), and their maintenance requirements (do they require extra watering, fertilizing, or pruning?).

Also note if the plants you already have provide food or shelter for birds and other wildlife. Birds native to your area have adapted to the available native plants, so having a wide variety of native plants will encourage a wide variety of native birds to live in your backyard year-round. In general, native plants grow better and produce more food and shelter than non-native ones. Also, non-native plants sometimes become out-of-control pests because there are few natural controls to restrict their growth and propagation.

Notice if the existing plantings on your property provide adequate cover and safe travel corridors for birds and small animals. Look for areas you can naturescape to provide natural shelter.

STEP 4: Consider your space requirements for work, entertainment, security, and comfort. Realistically decide how much and what type of space you need for each activity, and sketch these areas onto another piece of clear plastic that you can place over your property map.

STEP 5: List the wildlife that now visits your yard. If you have dogs or cats that live outside, you will probably attract fewer birds and other wildlife animals to your backyard.

Improving Your Naturescape

Use your property map, plastic overlays, and lists as the starting point for developing your naturescaping master plan. Ask the staff of local plant nurseries and garden shops to tell you about native plants and non-native plants that thrive in your area. You can also get lots of free information from your county cooperative extension service and your state Wildlife, Game, and Fisheries Agency (many of these agencies have developed detailed "backyard wildlife habitat improvement" kits). Some states even have funding to assist you in developing habitat for nongame species (animals with no regulated hunting season), and some states will provide native warm-season grasses and other plants for you to use. You can also write to The National Wildlife Federation (1400 Sixteenth Street Northwest, Washington, D.C. 20036-2266) and ask about their Backyard Wildlife Habitat Program.

Once you have gathered information about what plants will do well in your backyard, decide what existing plantings you want to keep and what plants you want to add. Keep in mind that you can make your naturescaping project as simple or extensive as you want—and you don't have to do it all at once. For most of us with somewhat limited time and means, naturescaping will be an ongoing project that will continue for years—and perhaps never be completely finished! Remember too that no matter how big your green thumb is or how much water and fertilizer you use, it just takes time for trees and plants to grow.

The information on the following pages will help you get started on your master naturescaping plan, whether you are starting from scratch, making major changes, or just modifying your existing plantings.

Starting from Scratch or Making Major Changes

STEP 1: Begin by planting a variety of native evergreen and deciduous trees along the edges of your property. These will simulate a forest canopy and provide food, shelter, and nesting sites for birds and other wildlife. They will also screen your property from streets and neighboring properties.

Plant deciduous trees on the south side of your house for summer shade and a combination of deciduous trees with evergreens on the west side to provide winter windbreaks. These should be native overstory trees that will reach 50 feet or taller.

Surround solitary trees with small shrubs (see Step 3 below) to provide ground cover and traveling corridors for birds and other wildlife. Allow enough room for tree growth when planting near buildings and overhead wiring to avoid having to severely prune or move a tree that gets too big for its space.

Suggested deciduous and evergreen trees: eastern hemlock, pitch pine, shortleaf pine, Virginia pine, white pine, loblolly pine, longleaf pine, slash pine, eastern red cedar (juniper), American beech, American elm, black cherry, persimmon, pin oak, red oak, white oak, black oak, live oak, red maple, sugar maple, shagbark hickory, sycamore, tulip poplar, ash, pecan, walnut, mulberry, American basswood, white basswood, arborvitae, birch, magnolia, sweet gum, and black gum.

STEP 2: Provide an understory layer by planting smaller flowering trees in clusters, not in rows, near the taller trees along the edges of your property. Irregular borders attract birds and other wildlife because they provide more "edge," more cover, and sometimes more food than rows of plants. Understory trees will reach from 20 to 50 feet. Mix several species of varying height, shape, and density, and select trees that bear fruit at different times of the year to provide year-round feeding opportunities for birds and other wildlife. Plant fruit trees that thrive without the use of toxic sprays.

Suggested understory trees: American holly, box elder, yellow buckeye, flowering dogwood, redbud, serviceberry, hawthorn, wild plum, sassafras, sourwood, hornbeam, cherry, myrtle, fringetree, Hercule's club, wild crabapple, and palmetto.

STEP 3: Plant shrubs and ground covers around the smaller trees to provide both shelter and food for ground-feeding birds and other wildlife. Select shrubs and woody plants that have multiple stems and reach no more than 20 feet. Buy plants that have several years' growth so they will mature quickly, and plant them in the fall to allow them several months of dormancy to acclimate to local conditions.

Ron Austing

Remember not to mount your feeders too close to shrubs because they make excellent ambush areas for cats.

Suggested woody plants: sumac, witch hazel, arrow-wood virburnum, wild hydrangea, spicebush, winter holly, elderberry, bayberry, blackberry, blueberry, dog hobble, mountain laurel, rhododendron, Carolina buckthorn, black raspberry, burning bush, chokeberry, corralberry, deerberry, gooseberry, leatherwood, bush honeysuckle, and huckleberry.

Suggested ground covers: cotoneaster, bunchberry, greenbrier, panic grass, and sunflower, bittersweet, dutchman's pipe, fox grape, summer grape, heartleaf, moonseed, trumpet honeysuckle, trumpet vine, cross vine, and Virginia creeper.

STEP 4: Although you may want to have some lawn for recreational use, large sprawling lawns are labor and energy intensive, and monocultured, manicured lawns do not provide much food or shelter for birds or other wildlife. Consider replacing some lawn area with flower beds, gardens, shrubbery, and natural landscaping. You may want to develop unneeded lawn area into wildflower meadows. Your local county cooperative extension service or state wildlife resources agency can help you choose warm-season grasses and native wildflowers that will make selected sections of your lawn wilder, more interesting and beautiful, and more attractive to birds and other wildlife.

Modifying Your Existing Plantings

STEP 1: Add enough new plantings to give you a wide variety of evergreen and deciduous trees, understory trees, shrubs, and ground covers (see Starting from Scratch or Making Major Changes, Steps 1, 2, and 3, page 43).

STEP 2: Add mulch around your trees and shrubs to keep soil moisture from evaporating quickly and to inhibit weeds. The mulch you add will eventually break down and begin forming nutrient-rich soil. Spread mulch 2 to 3 inches deep between and around trees and plants, but not directly against their trunks.

Suggested mulch: dried leaves, conifer needles, bark chips, and lawn clippings.

STEP 3: Replace non-native plants with native ones. Native plants are adapted to your area's soil and climatic conditions, often are more disease resistant, and are generally preferred by native birds and other wildlife.

Maintaining Your Naturescape

Lawn Areas: You can convert some of your lawn into a mini-meadow by mowing it just twice in the summer to control tree and weed invasion. Or you can mow the grass once every 2 to 3 weeks and set the blade at the highest cutting position. (If you live within city or township limits, check mowing ordinances before you create a mini-meadow or let your grass grow too high.)

Paths: Maintain mulched, stone, or concrete paths as walkways through your backyard when the vegetation is wet. Plant ground covers and shrubs along these paths to provide natural shelter for birds and other wildlife.

Pruning. Check with garden shop or nursery personnel to find out when and how to prune the plantings in your yard. Proper pruning prevents overcrowding, promotes denser growth, and produces more lateral branches, more flowering, and more fruit—all things that will benefit the birds and other wildlife. Be careful not to prune during the nesting season. Add your pruning debris to your brush piles to provide additional cover for birds (see Brush Piles, Stumps, and Snags, below).

Hedges: Create hedges from both evergreen shrubs (their dense needles and stickery branches make ideal cover and nesting areas) and thorny shrubs (they provide great escapes from predators and also discourage human interference). When pruning your hedges, vary the heights to provide a variety of shelter. Keep in mind that birds prefer somewhat unkempt, informal hedges.

Small Trees: Don't prune all the dead limbs—leave some for woodpeckers and other insectivorous birds to feed on. And don't take all the fruit from fruit trees for yourself—leave some for the birds.

Large Trees: Once a year mow under large trees to control unwanted seedlings. Also, maintain dead trees and limbs that are not hazardous—you may even "plant" some dead snags in your yard (see Brush Piles, Stumps, and Snags, below). Dead trees and limbs provide nesting and roosting cavities as well as woodboring insects for food.

Dead Wood "Plantings"

Not everything you add to attract birds has to be new. Try adding some old dead wood. Start thinking of brush piles, stumps, snags, fallen limbs, and leaf litter in a "new" way— with a eye toward providing shelter and food for wildlife.

Brush Piles, Stumps, and Snags

A brush pile is one of the easiest wildlife features you can add to your naturescape. For years I have piled fallen branches and cut Christmas trees along the fencerow in my backyard. They now make an impressive brush pile that is used daily by many ground-dwelling birds, including Eastern Towhees, Song and White-throated Sparrows, Mourning Doves, Dark-eyed Juncos, Northern Cardinals, and wrens. The brush pile serves as a refuge from predators and is one of the first places birds on my nearby feeders dash to when an alarm note is sounded. It also provides a welcome winter haven, and birds gather there regularly between foraging bouts at my feeders. The brush pile provides sanctuary for other wildlife as well, including reptiles, chipmunks, rabbits, an occasional skunk, and other small mammals.

Build your brush pile about 10 feet away from food sources and from other cover to help prevent cats from hiding in the brush pile and ambushing birds and small animals. Crisscross some big logs, stumps, and snags on the ground, leaving 8 to 12 inches between each piece. Add larger brush next and then smaller limbs, until you have a mound about 3 to 6 feet wide and 3 to 6 feet tall. Continue to add downed and pruned limbs and branches to your brush pile throughout the year. If your property is large enough, make several smaller brush piles instead of one large pile.

Stumps and snags provide excellent shelter for nesting, roosting, foraging, storing food, and hibernating. Decaying wood hosts a succession of invading fungi and insects that make stumps and snags much more suitable for birds that excavate nesting cavities, and the woodboring and wood-dwelling insects provide a convenient source of food. Open-armed snags also provide lookout perches for hawks and owls as well as for birds that hawk insects in flight, such as Red-headed Woodpeckers, Eastern Phoebes, Eastern Wood-pewees, and Great Crested Flycatchers.

Unless a large dead tree or its overhanging branches pose a danger to people, buildings, power lines, or other property, leave it and watch the parade of animals, including birds, that make it their home. If the dead tree is too tall to leave standing safely, you can cut down part of it, leaving as much of the stump as you can, and use some of the limbs to create a snag.

Woodpeckers (with the exception of the Red-cockaded Woodpecker, a federally endangered species that excavates its nesting and roosting cavities in living pine trees) excavate roosting and nesting cavities in dead wood. If the dead wood is soft enough, chickadees, titmice, and nuthatches also can dig out their cavities. Once a cavity has been excavated, skinks and other small reptiles may lay their eggs in it.

Snags with cavities provide nesting sites for secondary-cavity nesting species, birds that depend on other species or nature to create cavities because they aren't strong enough to do the excavating. Chickadees, titmice, nuthatches, Eastern Bluebirds, Great Crested Flycatchers, Tree Swallows, Prothonotary Warblers, starlings, and wrens frequent snags. If the cavity is large enough, American Kestrels, Eastern Screech Owls, and Wood Ducks may nest in them; screech owls may also use it as a daytime roost. Squirrels, flying squirrels, opossums, and raccoons may also call snag cavities home.

The lack of suitable cavities has been cited in countless scientific studies as an important factor in restricting the size of cavity-nesting bird populations. You can promote nesting and help increase bird population by providing dead snags on your property.

If you're sold on the need for a dead tree or two in your backyard but you don't have one, don't kill a live tree—unless it's an old deformed one that you were planning to cut down anyway. If that's the case, cut away the bark in a 1 to 2-foot-wide circle around the trunk, and watch the birds and other wildlife attracted to the dying tree.

A more practical option is to "plant" dead snags and stumps by inserting a large section of a dead tree or branch into a hole dug into the ground. This way you can pick the size snags you want and place them where you want (in a location good for viewing and photographing birds but where they won't damage anything if they fall).

When my friend Johnny Lynch created several shallow ponds for nesting ducks and geese on his 80-acre farm, he cut down dead Eastern Red Cedars (junipers) on his woodlot and "planted" the 8 to 15-foot skeletal trees in the water along one part of the shoreline of each pond. The dense wood of Red Cedar weathers well and takes a long time to decay, and these dead "plantings" have taken on new life as active perches for Tree Swallows that nest in boxes on shore and hunt for insects over the water. Red-winged Blackbirds use the dead trees as song perches from which to advertise and defend their territories, Belted Kingfishers use them as hunting perches when they scan the pond for minnows just below the surface, and American Robins, American Goldfinches, Cedar Waxwings, and other birds come to preen and rest in the open arms of the trees.

Keep your eyes peeled for dead trees in your neighborhood. Most folks will part with a dead tree or two just for the asking—and perhaps for an explanation of why you want them.

Fallen Limbs

Don't drag all your fallen limbs to your brush pile—place one or two in a convenient place in your backyard as a ready food source for woodpeckers and other birds that eat woodboring insects. Large fallen limbs also provide shelter and food-storage areas for squirrels and deer mice.

As they decay, fallen limbs absorb and retain water, creating a moist habitat that will attract salamanders and lizards. If you want to watch salamanders, place fallen limbs on north-facing slopes of a forested hill; if you want to watch lizards, place fallen limbs on south-facing slopes, which tend to be sunnier and thus warmer and drier than north-facing slopes.

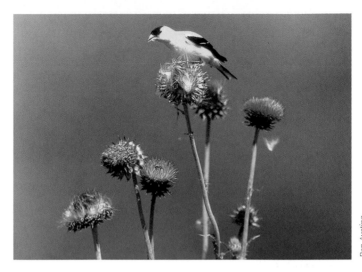

Ron Austing

Leaf Litter

Leaf litter releases nutrients back to the soil and offers a number of wildlife creatures shelter and food. Leaving leaf litter under your trees and shrubs will slow down the evaporation of moisture and attract insects eaten by wrens, towhees, sparrows, thrushes, and other ground-feeding birds. Leaf litter also attracts lizards, salamanders, and frogs. Gray and Cope's Gray Treefrogs hibernate in deep leaf litter.

So don't rush to rake all the fallen leaves from your yard. Leave some for the birds and other wildlife to enjoy.

Dust Baths

Dust baths help absorb excess oils on birds' feathers and discourage mites and other feather parasites. Sparrows, jays, robins, titmice, cardinals, and wrens regularly take dust baths.

Wet dust bath areas provide mud for Barn Swallows, Purple Martins, American Robins, Eastern Phoebes and other birds to use for their nests. Butterflies also frequent wet dust bath areas to "puddle."

You can create "natural" dust bath areas by scraping the vegetation away from a 3-foot-square sunny area. Till the top layer of soil to a fine consistency, and keep the area vegetation free.

You can build a dust bath by constructing a 2-foot-square wooden tray with 2 or 3-inch sides. Fill the tray with fine loose soil and some ashes, and place it on the ground in an open area.

Fred J. Alsop III

Water Sources

Birds need water as much as they need food. Although the food they eat provides some water, they depend primarily on clean freshwater sources in their environment. If you include even just one source of water in your ultimate backyard, you will attract the greatest number of different species. Birds of all kinds will flock to it to drink, bathe, cool off, and sometimes make mud for building their nests.

Offering water can be as simple as filling a shallow container and placing it in an accessible place, or it can involve digging a pond or constructing a living stream with a triple waterfall and lost lagoon. The most important thing is to have fun—don't make providing water so complicated that you don't enjoy doing it.

The best water containers are shallow (1 to 3 inches deep); if the container is deeper than 3 inches, provide rocks or perches in the deeper water so birds can rest and preen their feathers. Containers with shallow, gradually sloping bottoms are ideal.

Since birds don't have nonskid feet, make sure the containers have rough-textured bottoms. You can roughen up the texture by adding nonskid stick-on strips, or you can paint the bottoms with adhesive and pat on a little sand for traction.

Your first water container can be an upside-down garbage can lid, a shallow plastic bowl, or an inexpensive birdbath.

Once the birds spot your water container, they will continue to visit the container if you keep it clean and filled. Change the water daily, and scrub out the container with a brush and high-pressure hose to remove droppings, algae, and debris. Don't use swimming pool or other chemicals to kill algae in a container used by the birds—the chemicals will harm them. If you use soap to clean the container, be sure to rinse it thoroughly.

Place water containers in open areas that have at least partial shade—shaded areas not only keep the water cooler, but the absence of sunlight slows the growth of algae. Place the containers away from feeders so that seed hulls and bird droppings from these high traffic areas don't foul the water. Although the containers should be in open areas, make sure they are within 10 feet of protective shrubbery and low trees to protect birds from cats, hawks, and other predators.

If you live in an area where the winters are cold enough to freeze water, place a 40-watt lightbulb under the container or use one of the commercially available birdbath heaters. Don't use an aquarium heater because they are built for indoor use and may not weather well outdoors. Be sure to use grounded outdoor wiring to connect your heater to your household electrical power supply.

The heater does not create a hot tub or sauna for the birds amid the ice and snow—it just keeps the water from freezing so thirsty birds can get the water they need. Do not put antifreeze (glycerin), alcohol, or other chemicals in the water in an attempt to keep it from icing over—these chemicals are toxic.

Birdbaths

There are many styles of birdbaths available at nature supply stores, stores specializing in backyard bird feeding, hardware stores, larger variety stores, and garden centers. Traditional birdbaths have a shallow bowl placed on a hollow pedestal. Shallow dishes that hang from slender chains or rope have the advantage of being mobile and can be moved over and over until you find that perfect spot. Place hanging baths high enough off the ground to protect birds from ground predators, and tuck them under a limb that provides convenient perches.

You can make your own birdbath by tying a brick to the handle of a garbage can lid and placing the lid upside down on an upright cylinder of plastic or ceramic drain tile. The weight of the brick hanging in the cylinder makes the birdbath so secure that it will not easily tip over, even when a squirrel hops aboard.

Ground-level birdbaths appeal not only to birds that spend most of their time on the ground but also to those that live in understory trees and shrubs. You can purchase sunken or ground-level pools, or you can simply dig a shallow hole or series of holes and line them with concrete, tough plastic pool liner, or wooden or plastic barrels cut in half (cut off more of the barrels if the sides are too high).

Freeze-proof plastic water birdbaths made from polypropylene are extremely durable and can be used year-round without breaking in freezing weather. Birdbaths and pools made of concrete or ceramic often crack in freezing weather and do not hold up well over the years.

Child-size wading pools, which are often available at discount bargain prices at the end of summer, make great pools for birds. Just add rocks to make part of the pool shallow enough for birds, and use deeper parts of the pool for aquatic plants to make the pool a natural part of the landscape.

Pools and Ponds

Look at garden or nursery shops for booklets with ideas and specific designs for pools, ponds, recirculating streams, and other water-related features. Your library will also have books with plans, suggestions, and how-to-do-it directions, and you can find even more information on the World Wide Web.

If you have natural seep or wet areas in low places on your property, you might consider turning them into pools instead of fighting nature and trying to make the "swamp" into dry land. Using a little aquatic engineering, you may be able to turn these areas into natural "wet" lands, with shallow pools for birds and other wildlife at the higher end, with the water trickling down to the deeper end.

Creating larger pools or ponds may require some professional assistance. Before starting on an extensive project, check on your neighborhood and local ordinances for restrictions on waterscaping. Also check with your insurance company for liabilities related to having a pool or pond on your property.

If you decide to add a pool, use a length of rope to outline the shape and size in the location where you want it. When you get it positioned and shaped to your satisfaction, mark the outline with a lime "chalk line" or small wooden stakes, and start digging. Slope the sides of your pool so birds can enter the deeper water gradually. If your pool is at least 2 feet deep, you might want to stock fish for waterbirds (make sure the fish can withstand the top of the pool freezing over in an occasional Southern winter cold snap).

Running or Dripping Water

Many birds come to water when they hear running streams or dripping water. Using drippers, misters, waterfalls or cascades, or recirculating pumps will add the magical sound of water, giving you great opportunities to see species that might not come to your feeders. Many of the outstanding photographs in magazines of warblers, tanagers, orioles, vireos, and other treetop birds were taken when birds were initially attracted to the sound of water.

Drippers are easy to install, and their real value is in the noise they make. You can simply hang a garden hose over your birdbath or pool and adjust the tap so that a few drops per minute create a steady drip into the water below. You can also make a pinhole in one bottom corner of a plastic milk container, fill the container, screw on the lid, and suspend the container above your birdbath or pool; regulate the rate of the drip by loosening or tightening the lid. Saline-solution IV bottles used by medical-care facilities also make superb drippers. If you want to buy a dripper, look for them in stores that sell birdbaths.

You may also want to add misters to your waterscape. They have recirculating pumps and can be placed in birdbaths to produce a cascading fountain effect. They can also be placed on a tree branch or shrub above birdbaths and pools. Many birds like the mister's simulation of a light shower and will perch under its spray or, in the case of hummingbirds, fly back and forth through it.

You can use a submergible or recirculating pump to create a small stream with waterfalls and rills that invite birds down for a drink or cool, lingering bath. The decor can have a natural look or be as fancy as you can imagine.

Just for Hummingbirds

What beautiful and fascinating creatures hummingbirds are! These tiniest of birds (a nonmigrating Ruby-throated Hummingbird weighs only about 3.5 grams and measures about 2¾ inches) dazzle us with their iridescent plumage and aerial acrobatics. Hummingbirds, which feed primarily on the high-energy nectar of flowers, serve as the principal pollinators of many flower species. As hummingbirds and flowers continue to co-evolve, hummingbirds are increasingly found almost everywhere in the Western Hemisphere that flowers grow—including our backyards.

Once only people living along the Gulf Coast and in Florida could look forward to feeding hummingbirds year-round, but now it seems everyone in the Southeast has a chance of seeing wintering visitors from the western United States visit feeders from October to well into the New Year. Although only Ruby-throated Hummingbirds regularly breed in the Southeastern states, Bob and Martha Sargent of Trussville, Alabama, have banded eleven species of wintering hummingbirds. In the past ten years birders in my "northerly" state of Tennessee have recorded seeing five species—Ruby-throated Hummingbirds and four wintering species: Black-chinned, Anna's, Allen's, and Rufous Hummingbirds.

You can attract hummingbirds (often called "hummers" for the humming sound made by their rapidly beating wings) by providing flowering plants and nectar feeders. The plants they feed on are often too fragile to support even their lightweight bodies, so they feed by hovering in front of the flowers, which requires a high level of energy. It takes a lot of flower nectar (sucrose usually combined with glucose or fructose) or sugar water nectar to keep a hummingbird going. Researchers have found that hummingbirds normally consume several times their body weight in nectar and small insects daily, and if the nectar is calorie poor, they may consume up to fourteen times their body weight daily. When high-calorie nectar is available, the birds may have to eat only four or five times an hour, but when the nectar is low in calories, they may have to feed every four or five minutes. Most of the sugar hummers consume goes directly from their digestive tracts to their muscles, although some of it is stored as fat for an energy reserve to get the bird through a short summer night or long migration flight.

Planting a Hummingbird Garden

Hummingbirds find their food primarily by sight, and they seem to prefer tubular blossoms that are red, orange, or yellow—but they also visit flowers of other colors and shapes. Plant lots of flowering plants, both perennials and annuals, as well as woody vines, shrubs, and trees to attract hummers.

Your hummingbird garden will also provide food and shelter for the small insects hummers eat for protein and other nutrients. And hummers use the silk from spiders' webs to fasten lichens and other plant materials to their nests.

The following list will give you an idea of the kinds of plants to include in your ultimate backyard to attract hummingbirds. Use as many native plants as you can because they are already acclimated and will grow and propagate better and also produce more nutritious nectars.

Native Perennials

Beardtongue, smooth	*Penstemon digitalis*
Beardtongue, hairy	*Penstemon hirsutus*
Bee balm	*Monarda didyma*
Blazing star	*Liatris pycnostachya*
Blazing star	*Liatris spicata*
Blue sage	*Salvia azurea*
Fire pink	*Silene virginica*
Cardinal flower	*Lobelia cardinalis*
Jewelweed	*Impatiens capensis*
Obedient plant	*Physostegia virginiana*
Phlox, tall	*Phlox paniculata*
Phlox, wild blue	*Phlox divericata*
Rose mallow	*Hisbiscus moscheustos*
Royal catchfly	*Silene regia*
Wild bergamot	*Monarda fistulosa*
Wild columbine	*Aquilegia canadensis*

Annuals and Non-native Perennials

Canna	*Canna spp.*
Coralbell	*Heuchera spp.*
Dahlia	*Dahlia spp.*
Flowering tobacco	*Nicotania spp.*
Fuschia	*Fuschia spp.*
Larkspur	*Delphinium spp*
Geranium	*Geranium spp.*
Nasturtium	*Nasturtium spp.*
Petunia	*Petunia spp.*
Salvia	*Salvia spp.*
Scarlet sage	*Salvia coccinea*

Native Trees, Shrubs, and Vines

Azalea	*Rhododendron spp.*
Beauty bush	*Calliparpa americana*
Buckeye, dwarf red	*Aesculus pavia*
Butterfly bush	*Buddleia spp.*
Coralberry	*Smyphoricarpos spp.*
Hawthorn	*Crataegus crusgalli*
Lilac	*Syringa spp.*
Rhododendron	*Rhododendron spp.*
Trumpet creeper	*Campsis radicans*
Trumpet honeysuckle	*Lonicera sempervirens*
Tulip poplar	*Liriodendron tulipifera*
Weigelia	*Weigelia spp.*

Note: Many non-native trees, such as mimosa (sensitive tree), and shrubs that grow well in the Southeastern United

States also attract hummingbirds. Watch all the flowering plants in your area during your local hummingbird season and note which ones the birds feed on.

Hummingbird Feeders and Nectar

Hummingbirds seem to like red, and almost all hummingbird feeders have enough red on them to attract the birds like a magnet. If you feel you need even more red to help hummers find your feeders the first time, hang some red ribbons from the feeder or nearby twigs, or place the feeder near red flowers. Once hummers discover your feeder, they will be steady customers.

Clean feeders are a must, so choose ones that have openings large enough for you to insert a bottlebrush or toothbrush to scrub the inside. Plastic feeders are generally easier to maintain than glass, and they don't shatter if they fall. Buy several small feeders rather than one large one—it takes a lot of hummingbirds making lots of trips to empty a quart-size feeder before the nectar sours and ferments. And since hummers tend to be aggressively territorial, you will probably attract more of them if you provide a number of feeders and space them in open areas throughout your backyard.

Insects often compete with hummingbirds at nectar feeders. Ants love the nectar, as do several species of bees and wasps. Ants can be stopped in their tracks with a simple device called an ant moat, a small plastic "cup" with eye loops at the top and bottom that fits between the feeder and the hanger. Fill the cup with water or salad oil to prevent the ants from crawling out of it and reaching the feeder. Bees, wasps, and other flying insects can often be discouraged by using feeders with bee guards, small plastic baskets that attach to the feeding holes. Bee guards allow hummers to reach the nectar with their long tongues, but they prevent insects from reaching it with their feeding mouthparts.

Except for people who live along the Gulf Coast and have hummingbirds year-round, most birdwatchers don't maintain hummingbird feeders after the birds migrate south in the fall. But having feeders up and waiting when the first males arrive in the spring can be the key to having them stay around your yard for the summer. Check with the staff of bird-specialty stores or other birdwatchers to find out when the first birds will arrive in your area. Watching hummingbirds has become so popular that many newspapers run articles about their arrival and when to set out feeders. For those of you who live in my area (near Johnson City in Upper East Tennessee), the

Ron Austing

first male Ruby-throated Hummingbirds of the season arrive around April 6.

Sometimes after the first few weeks of the spring migration, the number of birds visiting your feeders drops off and you may think the hummers have deserted your backyard. Keep your feeders filled though because when the new food sources they have been exploiting begin to fade, they may come back with an appetite. And when the young birds come out of their nests in June, they will visit your feeders regularly.

Lots of people here in Upper East Tennessee think all the hummingbirds have flown south by Labor Day, but that is way ahead of their migration schedule. Many Ruby-throated Hummingbirds are still passing through as late as the third week of October, and they need as much food as they can get as fuel for their migrating flights. The farther south you live, the longer you can expect hummers to come to your feeder. Perhaps a good rule of thumb is to take down your feeders two weeks after you have seen the last hummingbird—but remember, leaving feeders up through October often attracts a visiting western hummingbird species long after the Ruby-throated Hummingbirds have left. And there's no danger of leaving a feeder up "too long" and enticing hummingbirds to overwinter where it is too cold for them to survive—the instinct to migrate is stronger than any nectar you can offer at your feeder.

Most commercial hummingbird nectar and nectar mixes contain red dyes that have been reported to be harmful to the birds' kidneys. Look for commercial nectar and mixes without the red dye. Or make your own sugar-water nectar by adding one part sugar (sucrose) to four parts boiling water—don't add red food coloring, honey (honey often contains a fungus that can kill the birds), or artificial sweeteners (they have no food value). Let the sugar water cool before you fill your feeders, and refrigerate leftover nectar.

You can safely vary the amount of sugar in your nectar and offer "stronger" nectar (one part sugar to two parts water) when the birds need more calories, such as just after they arrive in spring, when they are building up fat deposits before their fall migration, and after several days of unseasonably damp, cool weather. Don't worry—the birds will not "overdose" on the sugar; they just won't have to feed as often.

Replace the nectar in your feeders every three or four days, especially in summer. The hot sun has a greenhouse effect that quickly sours and ferments the nectar, making it unusable to the birds. Every time you replace the nectar, scrub out the inside of the feeder using a bottlebrush or old toothbrush and mild soapy water—but do not use strong household cleaners. Rinse the feeder thoroughly to remove all traces of the soap before you refill it. (For more about hummingbird feeders and nectar, see Nectar Feeders, page 16, and Nectar, page 26.)

Water Sources for Hummingbirds

Like all other birds, hummers look for a dependable supply of daily water, and they seem to especially relish taking baths. One December day in Oaxaca, Mexico, I watched a hummingbird hover over a dew-covered leaf for at least ten minutes while it brushed its breast and belly over and over against the wet surface and then preened its wet feathers. I have also seen several species stand in shallow pools and splash water over their bodies with their whirling wings.

I had read about hummingbirds visiting birdbaths, but I didn't see it for myself until I saw them enjoying a mister at a birdbath. The mister seemed to have a magnetic effect on the birds—they kept flying through it and perching under it, all the while working water into their feathers. Some birders have reported seeing hummers flying back and forth through lawn sprinklers.

You might want to include a mister in your ultimate backyard to attract not only hummers but other birds as well. Misters are inexpensive. Some attach to garden hoses and others attach to pumps immersed in a birdbath or shallow pool.

Other Backyard Wildlife

The naturescaping you do to attract birds will attract other wildlife as well, including squirrels, chipmunks, opossums, rabbits, skunks, bats, raccoons, snakes, lizards, box turtles, salamanders, frogs, and toads. Your life will be easier and your enjoyment greater if you welcome all of these creatures instead of trying to exclude predators or other "undesirables."

Some people have birds they just don't like come to their feeders. Starlings, jays, hawks, House Sparrows, and other birds you may not especially want to watch will come whether you want them to or not. You will probably react very negatively if you see a hawk preying on the birds at your feeders, but this doesn't happen very often, and it is part of the necessary balance of nature. You can "protect" the birds from hawks by placing your feeders within 10 feet of shrubs (be careful not to inadvertently provide ambush cover for cats on the hunt though; see Other Backyard Wildlife, page 59) or trees where they can take quick refuge.

Hawks and other birds of prey usually need an open area to successfully stalk their prey. Birds have keen vision and are very aware of movement, and it's very difficult for birds of prey to get close to a group of birds at a feeder without being spotted while they're still too far away to be more than a passing threat. When a bird sounds the "alarm" that a hawk is nearby, every bird at your feeders will sit dead still. Not until the hawk flys off and the "all clear" call is sounded will the birds begin to move again. Hawks are not as common as the bird species they may prey on, and you are most fortunate to have the opportunity to see one on your property.

If you don't want to feed jays, grackles, Mourning Doves, Rock Doves (Pigeons), and crows, surround your feeders with wire mesh that has holes small enough to keep out the "undesirables" but large to let smaller birds reach the food. Unfortunately the wire mesh won't keep out "undesirable" smaller birds such as European Starlings, House Sparrows, and Brown-headed Cowbirds.

Another way of attracting specific birds and discouraging others is to offer foods preferred by the "desirable" species. (See Food, page 19.)

Keep in mind that there are no "good" or "bad" birds or other creatures—each one is instinctively playing the role its species has evolved to play in the natural world. As birds and other wildlife accept your offerings of food, shelter, and water, you will be able to watch closeup how the various species interact. You'll be fascinated—guaranteed!

Squirrels

You will probably see squirrels as often as you see birds in your backyard. Squirrels have always been common woodland species, and they have become concentrated in the wooded sections of our urban areas as more and more forests have been cleared for houses.

Gray squirrels and the larger fox squirrels live in the Southeastern United States. Both species eat primarily herbivorous diets that include fruit, berries, nuts, flowers, seeds, buds, bark, mushrooms and other fungi. They occasionally eat insects, eggs, suet, and other meaty fare.

Squirrels are accomplished climbers and agile leapers, and they are smart. They make a living in the "real" world every day, and they have time on their side when it comes to figuring out how to get to the food in your bird feeders. Squirrels have no reason to think that food in their territory is "for the birds only." In fact, the food offered in bird feeders has given squirrel populations a boost! Squirrels live at least five or six years in the wild (well-fed backyard squirrels probably live much longer), and they raise two litters a year, with two to five young in each litter—so there may be a number of them living on your property.

You have three options when it comes to squirrels in your backyard: You can try to eliminate them altogether, you can battle them in an ongoing squirrel war, or you can learn to live with them. Trying to eliminate them almost never works. In most states squirrels are protected by law as a game species, and even during legal hunting season, most municipalities bar the discharge of firearms.

You can trap the squirrels in your backyard and relocate them (they probably won't survive in their new territory, especially if you relocate them during winter months). But the vacuum created by the removal of one squirrel seems to fill almost immediately with one or two newcomers. Besides, trapping is sometimes difficult, and you put yourself at risk by handling a trap holding an angry live squirrel armed with teeth that can crack nuts. And there may be legal restrictions on trapping and transporting protected wildlife.

Also, once you've trapped the squirrels, where do you release them? Several years ago two men were excitedly telling me their latest squirrel-elimination stories when all three of us suddenly realized that one of the men was releasing his trapped squirrels at a "perfect wooded spot" on the other man's property!

Poisons aren't a good way to eliminate squirrels either. Most poisons are broad spectrum and will kill any animal that ingests them, birds included.

Ron Austing

The bottom line is that there are no ways to effectively eliminate all the squirrels from a wooded lot. To help you put your ongoing squirrel war in perspective, I heartily suggest you read *Outwitting Squirrels: 101 Cunning Strategems to Reduce Dramatically the Egregious Misappropriation of Seed from Your Birdfeeder by Squirrels,* by Bill Adler Jr.

You can attempt to separate squirrels from the food in your feeders, but it's not easy and you will probably lose in the end. There will always be one squirrel that will figure out even the most ingenious barrier and get to the food sooner or later—and time is always on the squirrels' side. You can buy squirrel-resistant feeders that are encased in plastic-coated wire mesh or have metal perches and rims around the feeding holes (don't worry—the birds' feet won't stick to the metal in cold weather). These feeders don't prevent squirrels from physically reaching the food, but they do prevent them from chewing on the feeders and destroying them.

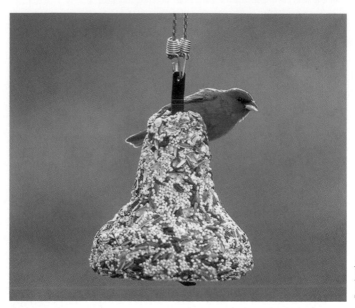

Ron Austing

Some squirrel-proof feeders prevent squirrels from staying on the feeders if they reach them; the Mandarin Sky Cafe model, made of Lexan plastic—the stuff bulletproof glass is made of, is the best one of this type on the market. Other feeders prevent squirrels from reaching the food inside the feeders by having a counter-weighted bar that shuts the feeding holes when a creature heavier than a bird lands on the feeder or a wire mesh cage that has holes large enough to let in small-to-medium-size birds but too small for squirrels. If you buy a wire-mesh cage model, make sure the cage will keep the squirrels far enough away to stop them from stretching their "arms" inside and reaching the feeding holes.

Unless you use the Mandarin Sky Cafe model, it's almost impossible to squirrel-proof a hanging feeder. You can discourage—or at least slow down—squirrels and other climbing animals by hanging large baffles over them or using feeders that have domed tops, such as Droll Yankee's Big Top model. You can buy plastic and metal baffles, both cone and disk shaped, at bird feeding supply stores or by mail order through birding magazines. You can easily make a baffle using a cylinder of galvanized stovepipe, but it's worth the investment to buy one that is the right size and readily attaches to the pole.

Here are some other strategies you can use in your ongoing war with the squirrels:

—Choose a spot on a limb at least 10 feet out from the trunk and 5 feet off the ground so very athletic squirrels can't jump out or up and reach it.

—Hang the feeder with thin wire. Do not use monofilament fishing line, string, or rope—all a squirrel would have to do is take one quick bite with its sharp chisel-shaped incisors to bring down the feeder.

—Alway put a baffle between the hanger and the feeder because squirrels can slide down even the thinest of wire with the skill of seasoned circus performers.

—I mount my feeders on poles and place a baffle right beneath each feeder. If you hang the feeder from a shepherd's-crook pole, you will still need to put a baffle on the pole to keep the squirrels from climbing it. Squirrels can shin up the skinniest of poles.

—Some people grease the poles with petroleum jelly, but I don't recommend it because it is potentially harmful to the squirrels as well as birds and other wildlife. Petroleum jelly can harm the animals eyes and mat their fur or feathers, reducing their insulating value.

—Fill your feeders with safflower instead of sunflower seeds. Safflower seeds have a somewhat bitter taste that the birds don't seem to mind once they get used to it (use a mixture of safflower and sunflower seeds for a few weeks before you switch to all safflower seeds). Squirrels—and black-birds, starlings, and Rock Doves—don't seem to like it (caution—the squirrels in your backyard may not know they're not supposed to like it and may eat it passionately!).

—Or fill your feeders with the "hot" new bird food—prepackaged sunflower (and other seed) laced with a film of hot red-pepper powder. You can also buy the pepper powder and sprinkle it on other bird food. The theory is that squirrels' keen sense of smell and taste will make them avoid your spicy offering, but most "desirable" birds will readily accept the pepper taste (many species feed on hot peppers in the wild). From my own personal experience and the experiences of others, I know birds will eat pepper-coated seeds but squirrels have mixed reactions. Some squirrels take one taste and immediately leave the feeders, and some squirrels relish the peppered mix as if it were just what they were looking for to spice up the bland seeds. You might want do your own taste experiment and see which side of the table your backyard squirrels choose.

Once you have accepted the fact that you will never completely get rid of the squirrels on your property and that you are spending far too much time and energy battling them, you might decide to just accept them as part of your backyard wildlife. You can still use squirrel-resistant or squirrel-proof feeders equipped with baffles and stocked with food squirrels don't particularly like, but don't get upset when they do manage to take a meal or two at your feeders.

You may even decide to feed the squirrels so you can watch them—after all, they are active, agile, clever, and cute. You can mix corn with more costly seed on platform feeders or set up a "squirrel-feeding" station away from your bird feeders and stock it with dried corn on the cob. Squirrel feeding is fast becoming a popular activity, and you can find a multitude of feeders designed to offer corn on the cob—from little wooden table and chair ensembles, where squirrels can sit quietly and eat, to whirls, twirls, and wheels you attach to an ear of corn so the squirrels turn end to end as they eat. Or you can easily make a feeder by attaching a large eyescrew to one end of a 24 to 30-inch length of light chain and a snap clip to the opposite end. Insert the screw into the large end of a corn cob and clip the chain around a tree or limb. The squirrels won't be able to drag away the corn, so you'll be able to enjoy watching them.

Raccoons

Raccoons are very intelligent mammals that are attracted to feeders, and they are not as easy to discourage as squirrels because they are larger, stronger, and perhaps have more manual dexterity. Raccoons can reach around most baffles and through wire-mesh cages to scoop food out of feeders.

You can make life harder for raccoons by placing large stovepipe baffles above or below your feeders. You can also limit the amount of food they get by filling your feeders with only enough seed to satisfy the birds, leaving little if any at the end of the day. Some people even resort to taking their feeders inside every night.

Raccoons are not as plentiful as squirrels, and you might be able to temporarily eliminate them from your backyard by trapping (Hav-a-hart type traps work well) and relocating them. Before you buy or set any traps though, check with local wildlife agencies to find out if any laws protect raccoons in your area and if you need permits to trap, transport, and relocate them.

You may decide after all that life is simpler if you just try to accept raccoons as part of your backyard wildlife and allow them a nightly share of the spoils. You will probably enjoy watching these bright, clever creatures perform their nightly antics right outside your windows.

As tame as they may seem once they have lost their fear of man, it's not a good idea to try to handfeed raccoons. They sometimes carry rabies, and their strong teeth and claws can cause serious wounds.

Mice, Rats, and Other Small Rodents

House mice, deer mice, rats, and other small rodents will feed at platform and sometimes hanging feeders and also on seed that invariably falls on the ground under your feeders. You will rarely see these nocturnal creatures unless you catch them off guard when you turn on the outside lights or walk through your backyard at night.

Southern Flying Squirrels may regularly come to your platform and hopper feeders after dark, especially for corn and sunflower and other large seeds. If you want to get a close-up look at these tiny creatures that have big, dark eyes, try standing close to your feeders in the dark. They will glide noiselessly past you, land on the feeder, and immediately run to the opposite side before getting close enough to the food to eat. They are often very tame and may let you get close to them. They may even adjust to having outside lights on, which would allow you to watch them easier.

Eliminating mice, rats, and other rodents can be a problem. Don't use poisons because they will kill all the creatures that ingest them, including birds. You can try trapping and relocating them, but beware of the risk you take in handling frightened, angry, sharp-toothed animals. If you rake or sweep away most of the spilled seed that falls from your feeders, you will reduce the food supply and reduce the rodent populations.

Attracting screech owls to your backyard will also help reduce rodent populations. I have several screech owl nesting boxes in my backyard, and I have often seen the owls sitting in the entrance holes at dusk while keeping a sharp eye out for mice. I prefer using this natural food chain of events to trapping or killing the rodents myself.

Predators

Predators, both native wildlife like hawks, foxes, and snakes as well as domestic pets, will prey on the birds you attract to your property. There is nothing wrong with predation—it is a natural way of life for species that do not eat seeds, fruit, or plants. Predators are not "wrong" or "bad"—they are simply playing out the ecological role their species has evolved to play in the natural world.

Even so, having a hawk show up in your backyard, finding the contents of a nest hanging out of one of your nesting boxes, or seeing a cat catch a bird at your feeder can be disheartening. Just remember that the predators (the wild ones, at least) are only providing food for themselves and their young—and the animals they prey on generally reproduce at a rate high enough to sustain losses and still maintain a healthy population. In fact, predators may even help strengthen the species they prey on. As biologists' studies have shown, predators often catch older, weaker animals and young, inexperienced ones, which reduces the number of birds competing for the food, shelter, and water.

Aside from hawks and owls, only a few other birds prey on the eggs or young of other birds. House Wrens sometimes peck open eggs of other species, and crows and jays occasionally feed on eggs and young birds.

House Sparrows and European Starlings, non-native species that were first introduced in the northeastern United States, don't eat other birds, but they are predators in the sense that they actively compete—usually successfully—with titmice, nuthatches, chickadees, bluebirds, and many species of woodpeckers for available nesting sites. House Sparrows and European Starlings are so aggressive that they sometimes build their own nests over the active nests of other species, break their eggs, and kill their young. You can thwart these "predators" by building nesting boxes to meet the specific needs of other species (see Providing Nesting Sites for the Birds You Want to Attract, page 38) and by providing nesting boxes without perches (perches make it easier for House Sparrows and European Starlings to defend their sites).

Male House Wrens can also be considered predators because they arrive in their breeding territories early and fill most of the available nesting boxes with "dummy" nests made of sticks. When the females arrive, each one will choose only one of the nesting sites, but in the meantime the males have driven off other species that will not attempt to nest in a box already filled with sticks.

Cowbirds act as predators in a different way. Each morning during the breeding season, each female lays eggs (sometimes more than thirty each season) in open-cup nests of other species. The unsuspecting "foster" parents often raise the cowbird young at the expense of their own young.

Snakes, raccoons, chipmunks, and squirrels all eat birds, adult as well as eggs and young, as part of their normal diet. Cats, both domestic and feral (the offspring of domestic cats that have been turned loose in the wild), kill many millions of songbirds each year. Estimates suggest that more than 30 million feral cats roam the United States, and if each killed only five birds (a very conservative guess) a year, we would be 150 million birds poorer. Add to this the number of birds killed each year by house cats, and the number is almost unbelievable.

You can give the birds you attract to your backyard an advantage over cats and other predators by doing the following:

—Place your feeders, birdbaths and other water sources as well as dust baths in the open, at least 10 or 12 feet from the nearest low brushy or shrubby cover so birds have a chance of seeing an approaching cat or other ground-traveling predator.

—If you have a house cat that goes outside, put at least two small bells on its collar to warn birds. (One bell is not enough because sometimes the sound is muffled—or the cat learns to move in such a way to minimize its ringing; but two bells will always sound a warning). Try to get your neighbors who have cats to do the same.

—If you have feral cats frequenting your backyard, try to get some help from your local authorities in trapping and relocating them.

—Keeping a dog on your property may help keep cats away, but dogs sometimes attack birds, especially young, sick, or injured ones that are more easily caught.

—Naturescape your yard so it has safe "traveling" corridors and patches of dense cover between the corridors that will help protect birds from predators (see Plantings, page 40).

—Place baffles around trees or poles supporting nesting boxes and feeders to thwart most climbing mammals from reaching the birds.

Photographing Birds

If you decide to try your hand at photographing birds, you probably want your pictures to look like the ones you see in wildlife magazines or the videos you see on PBS or the Discovery Channel. If you haven't already guessed, photographing wildlife in the field is difficult, so before you rush out and buy sophisticated equipment and plan trips to exotic places, start with a basic camera setup and practice photographing the birds in your backyard. Many professional photographers supplement their portfolios by photographing the wildlife that inhabit their own backyards because these birds and other animals are somewhat accustomed to seeing people in their "natural" environment, and their backyard feeders, water sources, dustbaths, plantings, and nesting sites provide camera-ready props and sets.

The information below about cameras, lenses, and related photographic items will help you get started on capturing birds on film. I suggest practicing with relatively inexpensive equipment and adding more expensive pieces as your interest and skill increase.

Cameras

Start with a 35mm camera with a single-lens reflex body that allows you to interchange lenses. Most 35mm cameras come with a 50mm lens, which is a good general-purpose lens but doesn't work well for photographing small subjects—you will need a longer, faster lens (see Lenses, page 70). The popular one-piece 35mm Instamatic cameras do not work for photographing birds because of their built-in small lens.

If you already have a good basic 35mm camera body, all you have to do is add an appropriate lens. If you need to purchase a camera body, you will have to choose from a multitude of available options. For a beginning photographer, simple is best. You can always add autofocus and the other "bells and whistles" later if you decide you need them.

I highly recommend using a camera with a TTL (through the lens) metering system. A good spot metering system pays dividends in nature photography where the proper exposure of the subject—not the background—is of prime importance.

If you want to capture the action and sounds of birds, you will need a video camera. The zoom lens format of available video camcras will give you a wide selection of focal lengths. Adding an inexpensive 2X teleconverter will give you even larger images and let you shoot from greater distances.

Lenses

With lenses, you get what you pay for, and the rule of thumb is buy the best you can afford. To capture the images of 5 to 9-inch songbirds, which nearly "fill the frame" of even 400mm telephoto lenses, you have to get within 20 feet. So in general, the longer and faster (smaller f-stop) the lens, the better.

Longer lenses, 300mm and larger, let you photograph from farther away because they decrease the apparent distance to the subject optically—they give you bigger images. A 300mm lens on a 35mm camera magnifies the subject six times; a 400mm magnifies eight times. Faster lenses (which have smaller f-stop numbers) allow more light to enter the camera, letting you photograph at faster shutter speeds—which is very important in catching the action of fast-moving birds. But longer and faster lenses (with f-stops of 4.5 and 2.8) come with higher price tags. Somewhere you will strike a balance between what lens you need to get the quality you want and what you can comfortably afford.

For most bird photography you need a telephoto lens in the 300mm to 500mm range to increase the size of the image, let you photograph the subject at a greater distance (perhaps as close as the animal will tolerate), and narrow the viewing angle to mask distracting background objects. A 400mm lens is perhaps the "standard" focal length.

I don't recommend buying less-expensive mirror lenses with fixed apertures. Although they are shorter, lighter, and somewhat easier to use, they have a fixed f-stop, so the only control you have over exposure is adjusting your camera's shutter speed. They also record any bright objects in the field of view, but these objects will appear as out of focus star-bursts on your final picture.

Zoom lenses let you choose focal lengths within the range of the lens. A zoom lens in the range of 100mm to 300mm will provide good backup for your longer fixed-focal length lens. To stop the action and get sharp pictures, shoot with the lens opened all the way (set at the smallest f-stop). This gives you the shortest depth of field, which puts your subject in sharp focus and the background out of focus.

No telephoto lens, no matter how long, can reach out and bring your subject in to the desired image size under all lighting and background conditions, and someday you will need a bigger lens—but the cost may prevent you from buying one. A relatively inexpensive option is to buy a teleconverter, a lens that attaches between your camera body and telephoto lens (either fixed or zoom). Teleconverters come in a variety of magnifications and magnify the image size of the lens you

Ron Austing

are using. For example, a 300mm lens coupled with a 2X teleconverter becomes a 600mm telephoto lens. Most teleconverters don't change the clarity of the image, and your camera will meter the light coming through the lens combination correctly. The price you pay for the increased magnification is losing some light from the film plane—a 2X teleconverter loses about 2 f-stops, but under most lighting conditions you can compensate for this by adjusting the shutter speed or aperture opening.

Another inexpensive accessory you will find very useful is a set of extension tubes, hollow rings of various lengths that mount between the camera body and the lens to allow the lens to focus closer than it normally would. Extension tubes offer the perfect solution when your long lens doesn't focus as close as you need because of your distance from the subject. Extension tubes won't let you focus on "infinity," but they will let you work in the 5 to 12-foot range where most of your pictures will be taken. Only the longest extension tubes reduce the amount of light falling on your film, so you meter light as you normally do.

Flash Photography

You may want to use electronic flash or strobe lighting later, but at first concentrate on working with natural light. This approach has the advantage of simplicity and gives you more flexibility in tracking and shooting your wildlife subjects. With flash photography you have to maneuver your subject into the narrow field where your flash is focused, and in

Ron Austing

daylight situations the artificial lighting can override the natural light, blacking out the background and making the subject appear to have been photographed at midnight.

So focus on using natural light now, and as your skill increases, experiment with flash photography.

Film Choices

Print films give you a little more latitude with proper light exposure than do slide films, and you can use film speeds ranging from 50 to 400 ISO (ASA) with good results. The faster films (higher ISO numbers) require less exposure time, which translates into faster shutter speeds and sharper images of active subjects.

I shoot mostly color slide (transparency) films for my teaching, lecture, and publishing work, and I get good results with 50, 64, 100 and 200 ISO films The slower speed films show almost no grain and are adequate in good light with a fast lens. Images made on 200 or higher ISO films show some grain, and the higher the ISO, the more granular the results. If you want high resolution and little or no grain, use films with a low ISO number. If grain doesn't matter, use films in the 400 to 1600 ISO range.

Don't forget about experimenting with black-and-white films. Although your photographs will lack the pizzazz and punch of color, you can create interesting black-and-white prints by shooting strong subjects in carefully composed settings that include a range of textures. And you can develop and print your pictures yourself if you invest a little in making a dark room, which can be as simple as a large closet in your home.

Whatever film you use, be sure to take a light reading every time with either the light meter built into the camera or a handheld meter. Avoid bright sunlight in the middle of the day when light on subjects is harsh and there are few shadows. Natural light is usually best early in the morning and late in the afternoon. Try shooting on overcast days— you may find that the color saturation of the natural light is surprisingly good.

One recommended accessory that costs pennies and is worth its weight in gold is a "gray card," a medium-gray stock card available at camera stores. Meter off your "gray card" to get average lighting conditions so your light meter will indicate the exact exposure you need to use.

Tripods

When shooting with a telephoto lens, you need to use a tripod. If you want a sharp image, the camera must be on a stable mount, and the bigger the lens you are using, the heavier the tripod must be.

Most good tripods come without a head to hold the camera/lens, and you must choose one to fit your particular needs. Be sure to buy a ball head, which has one lever that lets you move and pan your camera, rather than the standard tilt-type, which has three levers.

Blinds

Blinds (or "hides," as the English call them) are anything that can conceal you from your wildlife subjects. Using a blind you can make a "too-short" telephoto lens just the right length by getting both you and the camera closer to your subjects.

Even if you choose to shoot the birds coming into your backyard feeders from an open kitchen window, you still need to cover the window area so the birds will not see you and be frightened away by your movements. You can't get clear photographs by shooting through the glass in the window, so first raise the window and then hang paper or cloth over the entire area, leaving a port for the camera lens to poke through and a small opening for you to observe the comings and goings of your subjects.

Camera stores and photography magazines offer many types of portable blinds, but you can easily build one. Since the birds in your backyard are already accustomed to manmade objects, your blind doesn't have to blend into the background. I have seen great photos taken from inside cardboard boxes, tents, from under blankets, inside vehicles (they make great blinds as long as you stay inside them), umbrellas with "skirts" added, projector stands with adjustable telescoping legs with a tailored cloth over them, and many other simple blinds.

The basic requirements for a blind are:

—It should be large enough for you and your gear to fit comfortably inside, either seated or standing.

—It should be made of materials the birds cannot see through.

—No pieces are loose enough to blow or flap in the wind.

Birds accept blinds as part of the landscape in a surprisingly short time and quickly resume their normal behavior and activities. You can make them settle down even quicker by having someone walk with you to your blind and then leave after you are settled. Numbers don't mean much to most birds (crows and their kin are the exception—they can "count" up to 5), so the birds "loose count" when the other person leaves and behave as if both of you have left.

Props and Backgrounds

Birds are small, fast, and active, and you will be more successful in your efforts to capture them on film if you take some time to learn their habits and plan some backyard "studio" areas. Many birds take the same routes to and from nesting/roosting sites, feeders, foraging areas, dust baths, and water sources—just watch them for several days, and you will see some good photo spots. Searching for nests during breeding season will also give you clues for good photo opportunities.

If you have placed your feeders and water sources where they can be easily viewed from inside your home, you can set up your camera equipment, including a blind (see Blinds, page 73), and be ready to shoot whenever your subjects appear. Feel free to move or add more feeders or bird baths to get better camera angles—the birds will quickly adjust.

Before you start shooting, take a close look at the background in your viewing area. It should be simple, so it doesn't compete with the subjects in your photographs, and

Ron Austing

it should be well behind the subjects, so it will be out of focus and create a soft image that contrasts with the sharper image of your subjects. Shooting with the lens open wide will create a shorter depth of field and "soften" backgrounds, which will be out of focus.

Also make sure the background is natural, not something manmade. Manmade objects tend to have a repeated, geometric design that will pull the viewer's attention away from the subjects of your photographs. Strive for camera angles that show sky, grass, flowers, shrubs, and trees rather than a fence or side of a building.

You will want most of your subjects to be at about the same level as your camera lens. If you are seated in a blind, this will probably be 3½ to 4 feet above the ground, and somewhat higher if you are standing, so place some of your feeders, nesting boxes, and water sources about this height for photo opportunities.

Also provide some natural props in areas with good lighting and suitable backgrounds that your wildlife subjects can perch on to "pose" for photographs. Small sticks, limbs, and branches with blossoms or fruit placed near feeders, water sources, and nesting boxes will often become temporary perches that will provide interesting settings for good photos. These temporary props can be attached to posts driven into the ground, to the top of a spare tripod, or to the feeder or

Ron Austing

birdbath itself with wire, tape, string, or C-clamps. Change your props often to avoid a series of pictures of different birds all posed on the same branch or twig.

To encourage woodpeckers, nuthatches, chickadees, and other birds to "pose" on trees, press some suet or peanut butter mix into crevices or drilled holes on the backside of the tree. Then get into your blind and wait. Before long birds will be climbing and feeding in perfect camera view.

Identifying Birds

Placing feeders and a birdbath in your backyard will give you a good chance to observe birds close-up every day. And mounting birdhouses on poles and in trees will encourage birds to nest on your property, letting you see both young and adult birds.

Once you start watching the birds regularly, you will begin to readily identify cardinals, jays, wrens, woodpeckers, starlings, and other common species. But sooner or later, you'll notice an unfamiliar bird and want to know what it is. Here are some tips to help you identity that "mystery" bird.

Field Marks

Birders and biologists use field marks to compare one species to another and help identify an unknown bird. Each species has its own distinctive combination of field marks, which include behavior, relative size and shape, patches of contrasting plumage, bill size and shape, wing length and shape, tail length and shape, and sounds. When you see a new bird, take a close look at the entire bird and make notes about the bird's field marks (see What to Look for on a Bird, page 78, and Which Is It? page 80) Then look at the photographs and read the descriptions (starting on page 91) in this book for species with similar field marks.

Usually only one or two species will have a combination of field marks that are very similar. The more details you notice about your "mystery" bird's field marks, the easier it will be for you to decide which particular species it is.

What to Look for on a Bird

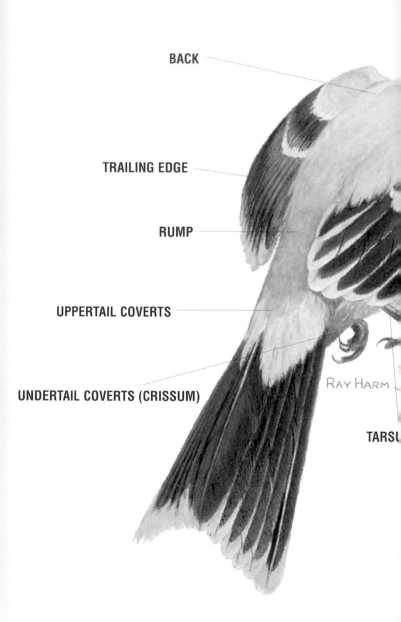

BACK

TRAILING EDGE

RUMP

UPPERTAIL COVERTS

UNDERTAIL COVERTS (CRISSUM)

RAY HARM

TARSU

NAPE

CROWN

FOREHEAD

LORE

UPPER MANDIBLE

LOWER MANDIBLE
CHIN
EAR PATCH (AURICULAR)
LESSER WING COVERTS
WING BARS

GREATER WING COVERTS

SECONDARIES

PRIMARIES

LEADING EDGE

Which Is It?

This **WHICH IS IT?** checklist will help you identify birds.

Where and When
Habitat
Impression
Comparison
Habits

Identification flashes
Sounds

Important details
Tail and wings

Where and When

Where refers to geographic region. Birds are among the most mobile and far-ranging species on earth, but almost all birds spend most of their lives within rather strict geographic ranges. So one important clue to a "mystery" bird's identity is where you see it. (For more about geographic regions, consult a bird-watching field guide; see Helpful Resource Materials, page 195.)

Occasionally an individual or small group of birds turns up in an unexpected location—much to the delight of ardent birders—but this is uncommon. If you are having trouble identifying a new bird and think it might be a "rare and accidental" visitor to your geographic region, invite an experienced birder to check out the stranger. In the excitement of seeing an unfamiliar bird, beginning birdwatchers often misidentify an expected local species.

When refers to the season of the year, another important clue in identifying a "mystery" bird. Birdwatchers plant trees, provide water sources, establish feeders, and build nesting shelves to attract both permanent and summer residents.

Permanent residents live in the same geographic region all year long. Blue Jays, Northern Mockingbirds, Eastern Bluebirds, and European Starlings are permanent residents in the Southeastern United States.

Summer residents breed and raise their young in one geographic region and then leave to winter in warmer regions. Ruby-throated Hummingbirds, Purple Martins, Wood Thrushes, Red-eyed Vireos, and Baltimore Orioles are summer residents in the Southeast.

Winter visitors come to a geographic region only during winter months, after their breeding season. Purple Finches, Evening Grosbeaks, White-throated Sparrows, Ruby-crowned Kinglets, Yellow-rumped Warblers, and Hermit Thrushes are winter visitors in the Southeast. If you feed birds only during the colder months of the year, you will see mostly permanent residents and winter visitors.

Transients pass through a geographic region only once or twice a year during their spring and/or fall migrations. Southeastern transients winter in Central America, South America, or the Caribbean and breed in geographic regions in the northern United States and in Canada, and we may see them in our yards for only a few days or weeks each year. Rose-breasted Grosbeaks; Bay-breasted, Blackpoll, Tennessee, and Magnolia Warblers; and Swainson's and Gray-cheeked Thrushes are transients in the Southeast.

Accidentals are birds that are not expected in a particular geographic region any time of year. Most new birdwatchers "see" many accidental species, but as they gain experience they realize they may have made erroneous or hasty calls. But look carefully—an accidental bird may just choose your backyard as the place to give the birding world a thrill! For example, one October a Green Violetear Hummingbird stayed for more than a week at a feeder in Asheville, North Carolina, about 1,500 miles north of its normal Mexican range.

Northern Cardinal Tufted Titmouse

Important details: crests ("topknots")
Cardinals, some species of jays, titmice, and waxwings have long, well-developed crests ("topknots"). Some species of flycatchers and finches have shorter, smaller crests.

Mourning Dove   Brown Thrasher   Wood Thrush

Important details: plain, streaked, and spotted underparts
Doves and some other species have plain, unmarked underparts. Other species, like thrashers, have streaked (the marks are longer than they are wide) underparts, while thrushes and others have spotted ("round") markings.

Habitat

Most birds live in environments that meet their specific requirements for food and cover. When you see a "mystery" bird, note the type of vegetation where it is—that will give you a good clue to its identity.

Impression

First impressions of a "mystery" bird will give you clues for comparing it with birds you already know. Notice if the stranger looks like a crow, jay, robin, sparrow, wren, dove, or other common bird. Also notice its approximate size. It's hard to accurately estimate a bird's size in inches, centimeters, or feet, but you can judge whether it's sparrow size or smaller (5-6 inches), robin size (9-11 inches), crow size (17-20 inches), or larger than a crow.

Comparison

Decide whether your "mystery" bird looks like a species you already know. If so, you have a head start in identifying it. Identifying a "mystery" bird involves comparing a newcomer with other species and eliminating species whose geographic ranges and features don't match the newcomer's.

For example, you may deduce that a new bird is a woodpecker of some kind because it looks and acts like a woodpecker. Make notes about its size, field marks, and the sounds it makes, and then compare it to the descriptions of wood-peckers in this book or a birdwatching field guide.

Habits

Your "mystery" bird's habits give you important identification clues, especially if the bird looks like another species. Make notes about how the stranger behaves. Does it feed only on the ground or only on the hanging feeder? Is it solitary or does it come and go with a group of similar birds? Does it walk (like many ground-dwelling birds do) or does it hop (like many tree-dwelling species do)? If it climbs trees, does it back down the

Northern Flicker   Yellow-rumped Warbler

Identification flashes: sharply contrasting feathers

The eye-catching flash of sharply contrasting feathers will help you identify Northern Flickers and Yellow-rumped Warblers.

Rose-breasted   Blue-gray   Red-tailed
Grosbeak   Gnatcatcher   Hawk

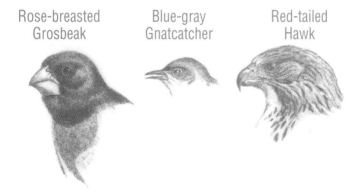

Important details: shape of the bill

Seed-eaters, like Rose-breasted Grosbeaks, have cone-shaped bills that help them crush seed coats. Insect-eaters, like Blue-gray Gnatcatchers, have small, tweezerlike bills that help them pick up their prey. Meat-eaters, like Red-tailed Hawks, have hooked bills that help them tear apart their prey.

tree in a hitching fashion like a woodpecker, walk headfirst down the tree like a nuthatch, or spiral slowly up and around the tree like a Brown Creeper? Does it cock its tail over its back like a wren or bob it up and down like a phoebe? Is it nesting in a cavity or in the open? Does it fly in a direct line or does its flight path undulate?

Identification Flashes

Many birds have colorful contrasting patches of feathers that produce eye-catching flashes of color when they are exposed. Sometimes these flash marks are enough to identify a "mystery" bird without seeing its other field marks.

Identification flashes include the white outer tail feathers of flying Eastern Meadowlarks or Dark-eyed Juncos and the white oval patches on the outer wings of flying Northern Mockingbirds and Red-bellied Woodpeckers. Other quick clues include the bright white rump patches of Northern Flickers and Red-bellied Woodpeckers, the yellow rump of the Yellow-rumped Warbler, the crimson crown of a Ruby-crowned Kinglet, and the brightly colored speculum on the trailing edge of the wings of many ducks.

Sounds

The songs male birds sing during the breeding season and the calls birds make year-round are often species specific. Professional ornithologists doing bird-census work may identify more than ninety percent of the birds in an area by sound rather than sight. Most species inhabit treetops, the darkest part of the woodlot, or other places where they may be difficult to see, but their songs and calls reveal their presence and their identity. Some species, particularly the small flycatchers in the genus *Empidonax,* are so similar in appearance that it is difficult to tell them apart with accuracy even when holding the bird in your hand, but their sounds are very different. Nothing beats listening to these vocal vertebrates, and as you learn their calls, you will be able to identify and more fully enjoy the birds in your backyard.

Sharp-shinned
Hawk

American
Kestrel

Eastern
Kingbird

Tail and wings: tail length, shape, and feather pattern
Some birds, like Sharp-shinned Hawks, have tails with
alternating bands of color. Others, like male American
Kestrels, have a subterminal band of contrasting color,
while others, like Eastern Kingbirds, have a terminal band
of contrasting color.

Ruby-crowned
Kinglet
Eye Ring

American
Robin
Broken Eye Ring

Golden-winged
Warbler
Cheek Patch

Important details: face patterns
Some birds, like Ruby-crowned Kinglets, have bare skin or
a ring of contrasting feathers around their eyes. Others, like
American Robins, have incomplete or "broken" eye rings.
Some species, like Golden-winged Warblers, have
distinguishing cheek patches or other face markings.

You can learn to identify the sounds of specific species by listening to the birds in your backyard, consulting descriptive phrases (mnemonics) in a birdwatching field guide, and listening to records, cassettes, CDs, and computer software available at your local library, bookstore, or bird store and through wildlife magazines.

Important Details

Try to get a good look at the "mystery" bird, and train yourself to look for details. Does it have a crest like a cardinal or titmouse? Is its breast plain, streaked, or spotted? Is its rump the same color as its back? How big is its bill? Is its bill cone-shaped like a seed-eating finch's, small and forceps-shaped like a warbler's or vireo's, or curved and hooked like a hawk's? Does it have contrasting patterns on its head like eye stripes or eye rings (complete or broken), crown stripes, or patches on its crown, cheeks, lores (the area between the base of the bill and the eye), or throat?

Tail and Wings

Your "mystery" bird's tail gives good clues to its identification. Notice the tail's length, shape, and any feather pattern. Is the tail long or short, rounded, pointed, square, notched, or deeply forked? Do the feathers have terminal or subterminal bands? Are there identification flashes along the sides, on the tip, or on the outer corners?

The newcomer's wings also give good clues. Notice if they are long or short, rounded, pointed, broad, or narrow. Also notice if the color contrasts with the bird's body color, like the black wings of a Scarlet Tanager contrast with its red body. Also notice if there are patches of color, bars, or stripes.

Using the WHICH IS IT? checklist will help you pay attention to detail, find field marks, and identify the birds. The more you use the checklist, the better you will become at identifying "mystery" birds. Identifying birds by their appearance and sounds is a satisfying skill you can use in your own backyard or wherever you go to watch birds.

Eastern Meadowlark   Dark-eyed Junco

Identification flashes: sharply contrasting tail feathers
The flash of sharply contrasting tail feathers of a bird in flight
help identify Eastern Meadowlarks and Dark-eyed Juncos.

Northern   Red-tailed
Bobwhite   Barn Swallow   Hawk

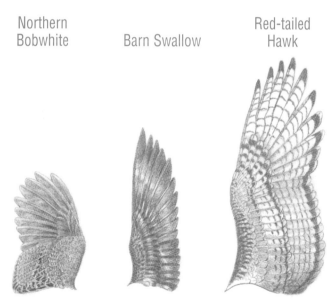

Tail and wings: wing shape
The wings of different bird species have adapted to where
and how they fly. Nothern Bobwhites, most songbirds, and
others that live in densely vegetated areas have short rounded
wings. Barn Swallows and other birds that hunt insects on
the wing (while in flight) have long, narrow, high-speed wings.
Red-tailed Hawks, vultures, and other soaring birds have long
broad wings with slotted "fingers" for slow flight.

White-throated
Sparrow

Red-eyed
Vireo

Wilson's Warbler

Important details: face patterns

Some birds, like White-throated Sparrows, have bold, striped crowns and eyelines. Red-eyed Vireos and other species have eyebrow (supercillary) stripes, while others, like Wilson's Warblers, have crown patches.

Red-bellied
Woodpecker

Northern
Mockingbird

Identification flashes: boldly colored wing patches

The flash of the boldly colored wing patches of Red-bellied Woodpeckers and Northern Mockingbirds, seen when the birds are in flight, provide good clues to their identities.

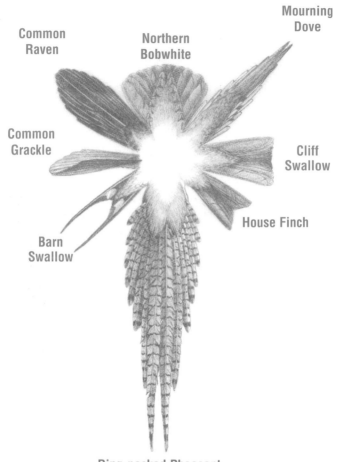

Common Raven

Northern Bobwhite

Mourning Dove

Common Grackle

Cliff Swallow

House Finch

Barn Swallow

Ring-necked Pheasant

Tail and wings: length and shape of tail

Birds' tails can be deeply forked (see Barn Swallow above), keeled (Common Grackle), rounded (Common Raven), fan-shaped (Northern Bobwhite), pointed (Mourning Dove), squared (Cliff Swallow), notched (House Finch), or wedge-shaped (Ring-necked Pheasant).

Brown Pelican

Pelecanus occidentalis

A marine bird, the Brown Pelican inhabits coastal regions where it can be seen plunge-diving into the water to scoop up fish. Often, these large gliding fliers travel in line formation with other pelicans, close to the surface of the water.

You aren't likely to see Brown Pelicans unless you live on or very near the Louisiana Gulf Coast. If you are lucky enough to do so, this Louisiana state bird will be a regular year-round resident of your back yard.

Fred J. Alsop III

Identification Flashes and Distinguishing Features:

With its long yellowish gray bill, streaky brown coloring, and low flight over the water, the Brown Pelican is unmistakeable.

Size: 48–50 inches (121–126 centimeters)

Color: Adults have streaked gray-brown upperparts, a blackish brown breast and belly, and black legs and webbed feet. Immature birds are brown with white underparts.

Voice: They are often silent but on occasion emit a low croaking.

Range: They are permanent residents along the entire southeastern Gulf and Atlantic coasts, as far west as Texas.

Habitat: They limit themselves to coastal saltwater areas, nesting on the ground or in low vegetation. Nests are built out of reeds, sticks, and grassy material. If on the ground, nests are usually built up 4–10 inches.

Eggs: They lay 2–4 white eggs; 1 brood per year. Both parents incubate the eggs; incubation takes 28–30 days. Fledglings leave the nest at about 35 days if the nest is on the ground, 63–80 days if the nest is elevated.

Food: They feed primarily on fish scooped up from the surface or plunged for from the air.

Habits: Gregarious birds, Brown Pelicans are usually seen in groups bobbing on the surface of the water or flying low, gliding and flapping in unison.

Cooper's Hawk
Accipiter cooperii

Cooper's Hawks look like large versions of Sharp-shinned Hawks, although female Sharp-shinned Hawks are the same size as male Cooper's Hawks. You can tell the two species apart by the shape of their tails: Sharp-shinned Hawks have have square-tipped tails, while Cooper's Hawks have rounded tails. Cooper's Hawks seem to have adjusted better to the fragmentation of woodlands and are more commonly seen than Sharp-shinned Hawks. The two species do not tolerate each other's company. Cooper's Hawks are sometimes called "chicken hawks," but they rarely disturb chickens or other birds that live close to their nests.

Cooper's Hawks will visit your backyard if you have pines and other conifer trees for nesting. They will feed on available small mammals and small to medium-size birds.

Ron Austing

Ron Austing

Identification Flashes and Distinguishing Features:

Look for the rounded tail that distinguishes Cooper's Hawks from Sharp-shinned Hawks. The crow-size female Cooper's Hawks are much larger than male or female Sharp-shinned Hawks.

Size: 14–20 inches (36–51 centimeters)

Color: Male and female adults have slate-gray upperparts with streaked and barred reddish underparts; their tails have white coverts and 4–5 blackish bars. Immatures have brownish upperparts with heavily streaked paler underparts.

Voice: They are usually silent, but when defending their nests they make noisy *cac, cac, cac, cac* clucking sounds.

Range: They are permanent residents in the Southeast except for Tropical Florida. Local populations increase during winter months, and their normal range expands southward with the arrival of migrating and visiting birds.

Habitat: They frequent woodlots and stands of deciduous or conifer trees. They make bulky nests from sticks and twigs and line them with chips of the outer bark of pines and oaks.

Eggs: They lay 3–6 dirty-white eggs marked with small, pale spots; 1 brood per breeding season. Incubation takes 24–36 days. Fledglings leave the nest 4 weeks after hatching.

Food: They eat small mammals and small- to medium-size birds (meadowlarks, jays, bobwhites, and doves).

Habits: They often perch in heavy cover below the canopy of trees and fly close to the ground in woodlots, which makes them difficult to observe. They sometimes soar on their short, rounded wings and long tails.

American Kestrel
(Sparrow Hawk)
Falco sparverius

American Kestrels, which are also known as Sparrow Hawks, are the smallest falcons in North America. They are the most common and conspicuous birds of prey in our area.

You can attract American Kestrels to your backyard by providing nesting boxes on poles or in trees (see Habitat, below). They will feed on available large insects, small mammals, and small- to medium-size birds.

Ron Austing

Identification Flashes and Distinguishing Features:

Look for the distinctive black vertical marks on the sides of their faces, their long, pointed wings, and long tails.

Size: 9–11 inches (24–28 centimeters)

Color: Males have brownish-red backs and tails, blue-gray wings, and streaked and spotted underparts. Females have brownish-red barred backs, wings, and tails and streaked and spotted underparts. Both males and females have black vertical marks on the sides of their faces.

Voice: When alarmed they make loud, rapid *killy, killy, killy* sounds.

Range: They are permanent residents across the Southeast except Tropical Florida. Local populations increase during winter months, and the normal range expands southward with the arrival of migrating and visiting birds.

Habitat: They frequent open and semi-open country and nest in cavities and natural holes in dead trees as well as in large abandoned woodpecker holes. They will nest in suitable boxes (at least 8 x 8 x 12–15 inches with a 3–inch entrance hole) mounted about 10 feet off the ground on poles or in trees.

Eggs: They lay 3–5 white to cinnamon-colored eggs with small dark-brown spots; 1 brood per breeding season. The female incubates the eggs; incubation takes 28–31 days. Fledglings leave the nest 4–5 weeks after hatching.

Food: They feed primarily on grasshoppers and similar-size insects. They occasionally eat snakes, lizards, and small mammals. They also prey on birds at feeders during winter months.

Habits: They are often seen perched on utility wires along highways. They sometimes raise and lower ("bob") their tails when perching. They hover with rapidly beating wings before swiftly swooping to snatch up prey.

Northern Bobwhite

Colinus virginianus

Northern Bobwhites prefer brushy areas, and you will more often hear than see them. Northern Bobwhites, which are also known as "quails," are managed as a game species with designated fall hunting seasons.

You can attract Northern Bobwhites to your backyard by providing brushy cover close to food and water and brushy "safe" corridors to larger nesting and foraging areas. They will readily come to ground feeders filled with cracked corn and small seeds and grains, such as millet, wheat, and milo. They also like water in a low birdbath or ground-level container.

Ron Austing

Identification Flashes and Distinguishing Features:

In spring and summer, listen for the distinctive *bob-white* whistle of male Northern Bobwhites.

Size: 9³/₄ inches (25 centimeters)

Color: These small, chunky reddish-brown birds blend with ground vegetation. Both sexes have distinctively patterned faces: Males have white throats and eye stripes; females have buff-collared throats and eye stripes.

Voice: Males whistle familiar *bob-white* song mainly during spring and summer; they make whistled *boy* calls year-round.

Range: They are permanent residents across the Southeast. Severe winters can decimate resident populations.

Habitat: They frequent agricultural areas, and plowing under cover crops and cleaning up fencerows may cause population declines. They prefer old fields, ungrazed grasslands, abandoned farmlands with brushy cover, and regularly burned open pinelands. They nest in hollowed-out clumps of grass; arches of grasses and weeds conceal their nesting cups.

Eggs: They lay 14–16 dull or creamy white eggs. Some nests receive clutches of eggs from more than one female and may contain 30–37 eggs; 1–2 broods each breeding season. Both parents incubate the eggs; incubation takes 23–24 days. Fledglings are precocial (capable of a high degree of independent activity from birth) and, like baby chickens and ducks, leave the nest within hours after hatching.

Food: They eat a wide variety of seeds, insects, fruit, greens, and buds.

Habits: They travel in coveys of up to 30 birds; the coveys split up in spring to pair and nest during the breeding season. Bobwhites often rise from underfoot on rapidly whirring wings.

Killdeer
Charadrius vociferus

Fred J. Alsop III

Killdeers are the best known inland shorebirds in the Southeast. Perhaps few birds have profited as much as Killdeers from the clearing of the eastern forests, and they are often found far from water on lawns, gardens, airport, golf courses, gravel parking lots, and railroad beds.

You may see Killdeers in your backyard if you live near cultivated fields or close-cropped pastures.

Identification Flashes and Distinguishing Features:

Look for a reddish tail that contrasts with brown upperparts when Killdeers are in flight. Listen for their distinctive, loud *kill-dee* call. Look for their "broken wing" distraction behavior during breeding season.

Size: 10$1/2$ inches (27 centimeters)

Color: They have brown upperparts, white underparts, reddish tails, and 2 dark bands across their necks and breasts.

Voice: They make loud piercing *kill-dee* or *dee-dee-dee* calls at night as well as during the day.

Range: They are permanent residents across the Southeast.

Habitat: They prefer open areas where they have an extended view and suitable ground cover, such as rubble, stones, pebbles, and gravel. During breeding season, the male makes several scrapes on the ground and the female selects one as the nesting site; their nest is sparsely lined. Killdeers sometimes nest between active railroad ties and on flattop gravel roofs.

Eggs: They lay 3–4 gray to pale-brown pointed eggs with black and brown blotches and spots; 1–2 broods per breeding season. Both parents incubate the eggs; incubation takes 24–26 days. Fledglings are precocial (capable of a high degree of independent activity from birth) and leave the nest soon after hatching; they can fly 25 days after hatching.

Food: They eat primarily insects; 98 percent of their diet includes beetles, grasshoppers, boll weevils, ants, caterpillars, dragonflies, spiders, snails, centipedes, ticks, and worms. They also eat crabs and crayfish.

Habits: They frequent dry land and mudflats but sometimes hunt shellfish in shallow water. Adults use a "broken wing" distraction display to draw intruders away from their nests or newly fledged young.

Rock Dove (Pigeon)
Columba livia

Rock Doves, which were introduced about 1621 by European settlers in Virginia, are now common permanent residents throughout the Southeastern United States, particularly in urban areas. Almost everyone has seen pigeons in a city park, making Rock Doves one of our most easily recognized bird species.

Ron Austing

While many birdwatchers don't want to attract Rock Doves to their backyards, others find them attractive and interesting. In some inner-city neighborhoods, Rock Doves may be one of the few species that visit feeders. You can attract them by placing small seeds and table scraps (particularly breads) on the ground or in large platform feeders that have plenty of room for landings and takeoffs. They welcome water in ground-level containers or low-pedestal birdbaths. They readily accept nesting lofts.

Identification Flashes and Distinguishing Features:

Look for their pigeon shape and white rump patches.

Size: 12½ inches (32 centimeters)

Color: Their plumage colors and patterns vary widely. Many have white rump patches, dark bands at the tip of the tail, and black inner wing bars.

Voice: They make soft *coo-cuk-cuk-cuk-cooooo* calls.

Range: They are permanent residents across the Southeast.

Habitat: They haphazardly build nests by placing grasses, straw, and debris on "artificial cliff" ledges, such as window ledges and crevices of tall buildings, bridges, and highway overpasses. Some live singly, while others form colonies.

Eggs: They lay 2 white unmarked eggs; they lay eggs throughout the year and raise multiple broods. Both parents incubate the eggs; incubation takes 17–19 days. Fledglings leave the nest 35–37 days after hatching.

Food: They eat spilled grain, animal matter, insects, greenery, and direct human handouts of bread and table scraps. They will come to ground feeders for seeds and table scraps.

Habits: In urban areas they have become so tame that they will eat out of your hand. Their strong wing beat places them among the swiftest birds in flight. They often "slap" their wings together over their backs as they take flight and sometimes as display behavior.

White-winged Dove

Zenaida asiatica

The White-winged Dove's rounded tail and large white wing patches, seen as a bold white edge on folded wings, distinguish it from the more commonly seen Mourning Dove. The distinctive *who-cooks-for-you* coo of White-winged Doves also distinguishes them from Mourning Doves, which make mournful coos.

Fred J. Alsop III

You can attract White-winged Doves to your backyard by offering cracked corn and small grains (millet, wheat, oats, barley) and black oil sunflower seeds on the ground or in large platform feeders that have plenty of room for landings and takeoffs. Like other doves, they welcome birdbaths and other sources of water.

Identification Flashes and Distinguishing Features:

Look for the distinguishing bold white edges on the folded wings of sitting and walking White-winged Doves. Also look for the white corners on their rounded tails.

Size: 11½ inches (29 centimeters)

Color: Males are larger and more highly colored than females. Both have brown upperparts with pale underparts; purplish-rose heads and necks; and red legs and feet. A blue ring of bare skin encircles their red-orange eyes; they have black marks below and behind their eyes. Their large white wing patches are seen as a bold white edge when their wings are folded.

Voice: They make distinctive *who-cooks-for-you* coos.

Range: They are native to desert areas of the Western United States, but increasing numbers live as permanent residents along the Gulf Coast and in Tropical Florida. They winter in the Upper East Coastal and Gulf Coastal Plains.

Habitat: They build flimsy nests of grasses and sticks. Some nest singly, while others form colonies, especially in suitable dense thickets of shrubs and low trees.

Eggs: They lay 2 creamy white unspotted eggs; 1–2 broods per breeding season. Both parents incubate the eggs; incubation takes 13–14 days. Both feed the young birds regurgitated seeds, insects, and rich "pigeon's milk," a granular fluid produced by the lining of the adults' crops (part of their gullets). Fledglings leave the nest 13–16 days after hatching.

Food: They eat a variety of seeds and grains (wild sunflower, doveweed, and small grains, such as milo, sorghum, and millet).

Habits They are often found in flocks, especially after breeding season. Some reuse their nests, while others dismantle them and "recycle" the materials in new nests.

Mourning Dove
Zenaida macroura

Mourning Doves, the most widespread and possibly best known doves in North America, have successfully adapted to a wide variety of "disturbed" habitats. The clearing of large forest blocks, opening of farmlands with grain and weed seeds, and close-cropping of grazing pastures have benefited this bird's populations. Mourning Doves are hunted as game birds during designated seasons.

You can attract Mourning Doves to your backyard by offering cracked corn and small grains either on the ground or on large platform feeders that have plenty of room for landings and takeoffs. Like other doves, they welcome birdbaths and other sources of water.

Ron Austing

Identification Flashes and Distinguishing Features:

Look for their pointed tails and heads that are "too small" for their bodies. Listen for their distinctive mournful coo. Also listen for the shrill whistle of their wings in flight.

Size: 12 inches (31 centimeters)

Color: Both males and females have brownish bodies with a pinkish wash on the underparts. They have long, pointed, white-tipped tails.

Voice: They make mournful calls of long and short cooing *oowoo-woo-woo-woo* sounds similar to an owl's call.

Range: They are permanent residents in the Southeast and have the widest distribution of all North American game birds.

Habitat: They often nest in trees and shrubs close to houses and sometimes build on top of abandoned robin or grackle nests. They build fragile-looking nests of twigs with minimal lining material.

Eggs: They may nest as early as February and lay 2 creamy white eggs; 2–5 broods per breeding season. Both parents incubate the eggs; incubation takes 13–14 days. Both parents feed the young birds regurgitated seeds, insects, and rich "pigeon's milk," a granular fluid produced by the lining of the adults' crops (part of their gullets). Fledglings leave the nest 14–15 days after hatching.

Food: They eat primarily small seeds, nuts, fruit, and berries. They will come to feeders for black oil sunflower seeds or millet.

Habits: Unlike other birds, doves drink by sucking liquid up their bills, horselike, without raising their heads. They usually mate for life. Individual pairs separate from the flock during breeding season and then rejoin the others. They fly rapidly in direct paths.

Eurasian Collared Dove

Streptopelia decaocto

These large doves, which are common in Europe and parts of Asia, are now well established in South and Central Florida and are extending their range northward. Although they prefer open woodlands and scrub or brushy areas, they also live in settled areas where people regularly feed grain to other birds.

You can attract Eurasian Collared Doves to your backyard by includng palms and other trees and shrubs in your naturescape, providing water, and offering grains either on the ground or on large platforms feeders close to the ground.

Fred J. Alsop III

Identification Flashes and Distinguishing Features:

Look for a black half-collar on the back of the neck of adult birds. Also look for the white lower half of their tails in flight.

Size: 12^1/$_2$ inches (32 centimeters)

Color: Both males and females have ashy-brown upperparts and paler ashy-brown underparts, with a pinkish wash on their breasts; their wings have blackish tips; and the terminal half of their tails are black on top and white underneath. Adult birds have a black half-collar on the back of their necks.

Voice: They make persistent *coo-cooo-cuh* sounds.

Range: They are well-established permanent residents in South and Central Florida. They are rapidly expanding their range northward and have reached southern Tennessee.

Habitat: They frequent palms and other trees but sometimes build nests on window ledges. They make fragile-looking nests of twigs with minimal lining material.

Eggs: They lay 2 creamy white unspotted eggs; several broods annually. Both parents incubate the eggs; incubation takes about 14 days. Fledglings leave the nest 13–16 days after hatching.

Food: Their favorite foods include cracked corn, sunflower seeds, and millet.

Habits: These tame doves often feed on the ground with other birds. They are generally seen in pairs rather than flocks. They frequent lawns, utility wires, and buildings.

Common Ground-Dove
Columbina passerina

Hardly larger than sparrows, Common Ground-Doves are the smallest North American doves, and their small size alone distinguishes them from similar species. These stocky little doves have scaly breasts and short rounded tails.

You can attract Common Ground-Doves to your backyard by filling platform feeders with cracked corn and small seeds, such as millet, oats, and wheat. They are highly attracted to water in birdbaths and shallow pools.

Ron Austing

Identification Flashes and Distinguishing Features:

Look for the flash of chestnut-brown in their outer wings when they are in flight. Also look for the black tails of the males.

Size: 6¹/₂ inches (17 centimeters)

Color: Both males and females have brown upperparts, with some black spots on their backs and wings, and pinkish-brown underparts. Their dark bills have pinkish-red tips. Their legs and feet are pink to yellow.

Voice: They make repeated soft, rising *coo-up* sounds.

Range: They are permanent residents in the East Gulf Coastal Plain, the South Atlantic Coastal Plain, and all of Florida. They frequent backyards in Florida and may stray to feeders in backyards in other states farther north.

Habitat: They prefer open, dry ground and nest on the ground or close to it. They make shallow nesting cups from small twigs, grasses, and rootlets.

Eggs: They lay 2 white unmarked eggs; 2 or more broods per breeding season. Both parents incubate the eggs; incubation takes 12–14 days. Fledglings leave the nest about 14 days after hatching.

Food: Their favorite foods include millet, hemp, and cracked corn. Also feed on grass seeds, weed seeds, small berries, and insects.

Habits: They may pair for life. They walk briskly on their short legs and nod their heads while walking. They are quite tame and may allow you to get within a few strides' length. They fly in a zigzag pattern on dry-sounding wings.

Common Nighthawk
Chordeiles minor

Often called bullbats in the Southeastern United States, Common Nighthawks are the most frequently seen members of the nightjar family, which includes Whippoor-wills and Chuck-will's-widows. They become active around dusk, and their nocturnal songs are frequently heard as they fly over houses on summer nights. They feed on the wing, sweeping up insects into their cavernous mouths.

You may see them in your backyard near security lights.

Ron Austing

Identification Flashes and Distinguishing Features:

When they are in flight, look for the bold white bars at the edge of their long, pointed wings.

Size: 9¹/₂ inches (24 centimeters)

Color: Both males and females have gray or gray-brown bodies; males have white throats and a white bar across their tails. They have a bold white bar toward the tip of each long, pointed wing.

Voice: They make froglike, nasal *peent* calls.

Range: They are common summer residents in the Southeast, especially in urban areas. They migrate in late summer to their wintering grounds south of the United States. Huge flocks can often be seen flying across late-afternoon skies in the Southeastern states.

Habitat: They prefer bare or sparsely vegetated ground, graveled areas, and even flattop gravel roofs where their drab plumage blends into the background. They do not build nests but lay their eggs directly on the ground or gravel surface.

Eggs: They lay 2 creamy white to buff olive eggs that are heavily speckled with brown and gray. The female incubates the eggs; incubation takes about 19 days. Fledglings leave the nest about 21 days after hatching.

Food: They eat primarily insects, including flying ants, mosquitoes, beetles, and moths.

Habits: They hunt mostly at night but are also seen during the day. Common Nighthawks and other nightjars sit parallel to their perches rather than perpendicular, as is common with other bird species. They are often seen sleeping on fence posts, large utility wires, or tree branches. They frequently feed on insects attracted to bright security lights in urban settings.

Eastern Screech-Owl
Otus asio

Perhaps the most common owl in the Southeast, small Eastern Screech-Owls have distinctive ear tufts that can be raised or lowered to give them a broad, round-headed appearance. These owls are attracted to trees, including dead or partially dead ones, with suitable nesting/roosting cavities.

You can attract Eastern Screech-Owls to your backyard by providing suitable nesting/roosting boxes (see Habitat, below). They will feed on available large insects and small animals.

Ron Austing

Identification Flashes and Distinguishing Features:

Look for their distinctive ear tufts and small bodies.

Size: 8 1/2 inches (22 centimeters)

Color: They may have an overall covering of reddish, brown, or gray; those with reddish plumage are most commonly seen in the Southeast. They have dark streaks below their yellow eyes.

Voice: Their call is not a screech (as their name implies) but rather a low, long trill on one pitch or a series of quavering whistles that descend in pitch.

Range: They are permanent residents in the Southeast.

Habitat: They prefer to roost in tree cavities or crevices in buildings during the day. They nest and roost in the same cavities, often choosing abandoned flicker and Pileated Woodpecker holes. They will nest in suitable boxes (9 x 9 x 16 inches with a 3-inch hole cut 3 inches below the top) mounted at least 10 feet above the ground in wooded areas. They do not build nests; they lay their eggs directly on the wood chips, leaves, and other debris on the cavity floor.

Eggs: They lay 2–7 round, white eggs at 2–3 day intervals; 1 brood per breeding season. The female incubates the eggs, and the male may stay in the cavity with her during the day; incubation takes about 26 days. Fledglings leave the nest about 28 days after hatching.

Food: They feed on a wide variety of large insects, fish, and animals, including small rodents, small reptiles, amphibians, small birds, crayfish, and earthworms.

Habits: They are nocturnal and become active about dusk. Although they are not attracted to bird-feeder fare, they may hunt mice that eat at the feeders at night. You will more often hear than see Eastern Screech-Owls. By imitating their call, you may be able to get the birds to keep calling and come closer into view.

Ron Austing

Ruby-throated Hummingbird
Archilochus colubris

Ruby-throated Hummingbirds are the smallest breeding birds in the Southeast. They are so small and active that you may mistake them for large insects, such as bumblebees and hawk (hummingbird) moths.

You can easily attract these fearless winged "mites" to your backyard by providing water, offering nectar feeders (see Just for Hummingbirds, page 53), and including plants that bear red, orange, or yellow tube-shaped flowers in your naturescape.

Ron Austing

Identification Flashes and Distinguishing Features:

Look for the flash of their iridescent green and red feathers as they dart around flowers and feeders. Listen for the humming sound of their wings, which beat up to 75 strokes per second.

Size: 3³/₄ inches (10 centimeters)

Color: Males are metallic green above and white below, with dusky green sides, dark forked tails, black chins, and brilliantly colored throats that flash ruby red when the sunlight catches them at the right angle and otherwise appear black. Females are metallic green above and white below, with a buffy wash on their sides. They have green tails tipped with blackish feathers; the three outermost tail feathers have white tips.

Voice: They make excited, high-pitched squeaks and twitters.

Range: They are summer residents throughout the Southeast, arriving as early as March along the Gulf Coast and departing in October. Some winter in Tropical Florida.

Habitat: Females construct their nests using plant down, flower petals, fibers, and bud scales; they decorate the outside with green and gray lichens held on by spider's silk or webs from tent caterpillars' nests. The nests are attached with spider's silk to tops of gently slanted branches; completed nests resemble lichen-covered knots approximately 1¹/₂ inches in diameter.

Eggs: They lay 2 pea-size white eggs; 2–3 broods each breeding season. The female incubates the eggs; incubation takes 14–16 days. Fledglings leave the nest 20–22 days after hatching.

Food: They feed on nectar and tree sap, sugar-water nectar in feeders, and small insects.

Habits: They are commonly found wherever there are flowers, and they are especially attracted to red flowers and feeders. They hover while feeding and are the only birds that can fly backward. They actively defend their feeding territories from other hummingbirds as well as much larger birds.

Ron Austing

Rufous Hummingbird
Selasphorus rufus

Rufous Hummingbirds, which breed in the Northwestern United States from Oregon, Idaho, and western Montana north to southeastern coastal Alaska, have been showing up increasingly more frequently in the Southeast as winter visitors. They often arrive in October and may stay until the following spring breeding season. If you live north of Tropical Florida and see a hummingbird at your nectar feeder after the Ruby-throated Hummingbirds have departed (usually by mid-October), your visitor is probably a Rufous Hummingbird.

Joe Riser

You can attract Rufous Hummingbirds by offering water and sugar-water nectar (see Just for Hummingbirds, page 53). Be sure to keep your feeders cleaned and filled for several weeks after your last Ruby-throated Hummingbird has departed to catch the hungry eye of the winter visitors.

Identification Flashes and Distinguishing Features:

Look for the distinguishing rufous underparts and backs of males. Listen for the low, quiet humming sound of the wings.

Size: 3³/₄ inches (10 centimeters)

Color: Male Rufous Hummingbirds are the only North American hummingbirds with both rufous upperparts and underparts; they have green crowns and white breasts with iridescent scarlet-burnished gold gorgets (throat and upper breast areas). Females have iridescent green upperparts and white underparts with faded rust-colored sides.

Voice: They make *chup, chup* whistles.

Range: They are uncommon fall, winter, and early spring visitors in the Southeast.

Habitat: Females construct nests using plant down, flower petals, fibers, and bud scales; they decorate the outside with green and gray lichens held on by spider's silk or webs from tent caterpillars' nests. The nests are attached with spider's silk to tops of gently slanted branches; completed nests resemble a lichen-covered knot approximately 1¹/₂ inches in diameter.

Eggs: They lay 2 white unmarked eggs; 1 brood per breeding season. The female incubates the eggs; length of incubation has not been verified. Fledglings leave the nest 20 days after hatching.

Food: They feed on nectar and tree sap, sugar-water nectar in feeders, and small insects.

Habits: They are commonly found wherever there are flowers, and they are especially attracted to red flowers and feeders. They hover while feeding and are the only birds that can fly backward. They actively defend their feeding territories from other hummingbirds as well as much larger birds.

Red-headed Woodpecker
Melanerpes erythrocephalus

These medium-size woodpeckers have suffered population declines where aggressive European Starlings have caused them to abandon their nesting cavities. Their reduced populations and patchy distribution makes them relatively uncommon, but their habit of feeding along roads makes them the woodpecker most frequently killed by vehicles in the Southeast.

You can attract them by providing dead snags or nesting boxes (see Habitat, below) and offering sunflower seeds, raisins, or suet.

Ron Austing

Identification Flashes and Distinguishing Features:

The contrast between their red heads and necks, white underparts, and jet-black backs, wings, and tails makes it hard to miss adult Red-headed Woodpeckers.

Size: 9–9³/₄ inches (23–25 centimeters)

Color: Adult males and females have bright scarlet-red head, neck, and throat areas; juveniles have ashy-brown heads. They have snowy white underparts, rumps, wing patches, and secondary wing feathers; jet-black backs, tails, and wings.

Voice: They make loud *queer, queer, queer* or *queark* sounds.

Range: They are permanent residents throughout the Southeast except Tropical Florida.

Habitat: They prefer open stands of trees with little undergrowth. Both parents excavate the nesting cavity, choosing a dead tree, dead stub of a live tree, utility pole, or fence post. They occasionally nest in manmade boxes (5 x 7 x 16 inches with a 2-inch hole cut 3 inches below the top) mounted 10 feet above the ground in a wooded area and filled with sawdust, which allows the woodpeckers to "excavate" their cavity.

Eggs: They lay 4–7 oval white eggs; 1–2 broods per breeding season. Both parents incubate the eggs; incubation takes about 14 days. Fledglings leave the nest 24–27 days after hatching.

Food: They drill for wood-boring grubs and insects; forage on the ground for beetles, ants, wasps, other insects, and fallen seeds. Like flycatchers, they also perch and wait for flying insects. They feed on fruit, berries, and large nuts in fall, and they store winter foods, especially acorns, beechnuts, and corn. They will come to feeders for cracked corn, sunflower seeds, raisins, suet, and suet mixes.

Habits: They frequent parklike stands of large trees in rural and urban areas, large scattered deciduous trees in open grasslands and agricultural areas, and dead trees in swampy or burned-over areas. They catch insects in midair, flycatcher style.

Ron Austing

Red-bellied Woodpecker

Melanerpes carolinus

They are perhaps the most common medium-size woodpeckers found in the Southeast, and their noisy tappings and frequent calls announce their presence. They are often mistakenly called "red-headed woodpeckers" (see page 107) because their heads have a lot of red and their namesake red belly patches are often hidden from view.

You can attract Red-bellied Woodpeckers to your backyard by filling feeders with black oil sunflower seeds, corn, suet, or peanut butter-suet mixes.

Fred J. Alsop III

Ron Austing

Identification Flashes and Distinguishing Features:

Look for the distinguishing "zebra-striped" bars on their backs and their bold white rumps and wing spots when they're in flight.

Size: 9¼ inches (24 centimeters)

Color: Males have red foreheads, crowns, and napes. Females have only red napes; the rest of their head areas are pale gray. Both sexes have pale gray on the sides of their faces; black-and-white barred wings, upperparts, and central tail feathers; and a reddish wash on their lower bellies in front of and between their legs. Their white rumps and wing patches are conspicuous in flight.

Voice: They make rolling *churrrrr, churrrrr* and abrupt *chuck, chuck, chuck* sounds.

Range: They are permanent residents throughout the Southeast.

Habitat: They frequent lawns and gardens wherever there are shrubs and trees. They are common in woodlands, particularly areas of bottomland hardwoods and swamps, and they are readily found in pinelands and areas of mixed pines and hardwoods with large trees. They are also common in urban areas that have large trees and in wooded farmlands. Both parents excavate the nesting cavity in a dead stub or soft-wooded deciduous tree. They sometimes nest in utility poles, fence posts, or abandoned cavities of other woodpeckers.

Eggs: They lay 3–8 unspotted white eggs; 1–2 broods per breeding season. Both parents incubate the eggs—the female during the day and the male during the night; incubation takes 12–14 days. Fledglings leave the nest 24–26 days after hatching.

Food: They drill for wood-boring insects and larvae and forage on the ground for beetles, ants, and grasshoppers. They also feed on nuts, berries, and fruit. They will come to feeders for sunflower seeds, corn, suet, and peanut butter-suet mixes.

Habits: They make noisy, loud tappings and frequent calls that seldom go unnoticed.

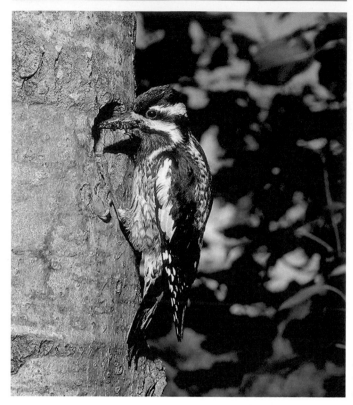

Ron Austing

Yellow-bellied Sapsucker

Sphyrapicus varius

Before you see these medium-size woodpeckers, you may notice neat horizontal rows of ¼-inch feeding wells in trees in your backyard—sure signs that a sapsucker has been at work. While people in the timber business may not like the small regular holes left by sapsuckers, they probably do appreciate the fact that sapsuckers feed on many insects that are injurious to trees. Unlike other woodpeckers, sapsuckers have brushlike tongues that are adapted to licking tree sap. Other birds feed at the sap wells that are drilled and maintained by sapsuckers.

You can attract Yellow-bellied Sapsuckers to your backyard by including sugar maple, apple, and pear trees in your naturescape and by filling feeders with suet or suet mixes.

Identification Flashes and Distinguishing Features:

Look for their straw-yellow underparts; white rumps and shoulder patches; and black breast bibs, wings, and tails.

Size: 8 1/2 inches (22 centimeters)

Color: Males have red chins and throats; females have white chins and throats. Both sexes have black breast bibs, wings, and tails; and large, white shoulder patches readily seen on their folded wings. Their backs are mottled white, brown, and black in a lichenlike pattern; their bellies have a yellowish wash.

Voice: Most often they make catlike, nasal mewing sounds.

Range: They are breeding birds in the Southern Blue Ridge area of eastern Tennessee, western North Carolina, and northwestern Georgia. They are winter visitors throughout the Southeast.

Habitat: They frequent both deciduous and coniferous trees. Both parents excavate a gourd-shaped cavity in a soft northern hardwood tree, such as yellow birch.

Eggs: They lay 4–7 white eggs;1 brood per breeding season. Both parents incubate the eggs—the female during the day, the male during the night; incubation takes 12–14 days. Fledglings leave the nest 25–29 days after hatching.

Food: They lick tree sap, a major part of their diet, with their brushlike tongues. They feed on insects attracted to their sap wells as well as insects found in other places. They also feed on fruit and berries. They will come to feeders for suet, suet mixes, or sugar-water nectar.

Habits: They drill feeding-wells in more than 275 species of trees and return frequently to lick the sap with their brushlike tongues. They also catch insects on the wing, flycatcher style.

Fred J. Alsop III

Downy Woodpecker

Picoides pubescens

Downy Woodpeckers, the smallest and most common woodpeckers in the Southeast, look like small Hairy Woodpeckers with sparrow-size bills. Their fondness for small broken woodlots makes them at home in cities as well as in suburbs and rural settings.

You can attract Downy Woodpeckers by providing nesting boxes (see Habitat, below) and by offering black oil sunflower seeds, suet, peanut butter, nuts, and table scraps, especially cornbread and doughnuts.

Ron Austing

Ron Austing

Identification Flashes and Distinguishing Features:

Look for their small size and white backs, which help distinguish them from other woodpeckers.

Size: 6–6³/₄ inches (15–17 centimeters)

Color: Adult males and females have black-and-white heads, but males have a red patch on the back of their heads. Both have black wings with many white spots, black tails with white outer tail feathers marked by blackish dots, and white underparts and backs.

Voice: They make sharp *plik* calls and a downward whinnying that sounds like a small horse.

Range: They are permanent residents throughout the Southeast.

Habitat: They (especially males) frequent small saplings and smaller branches of trees that won't support the weight of larger woodpeckers. Both parents dig a gourd-shaped nesting cavity with a 1¹/₄–inch entrance hole. They usually nest in dead stubs, although sometimes in living trees or fence posts. Occasionally they nest in manmade boxes (5 x 5 x 10 inches with 1¹/₄–inch hole cut 2 inches below the top) mounted at least 8 feet above the ground in a wooded area and filled with sawdust, which allows the woodpeckers to "excavate" their nesting cavity.

Eggs: They lay 3–6 oval white eggs; 2 broods per breeding season. Both parents incubate the eggs—the female during the day, the male during the night; incubation takes about 12 days. Fledglings leave the nest 21–24 days after hatching.

Food: They feed on wood-boring, fruit-boring, and nut/seed-boring insects as well as grasshoppers, spiders, and snails. They also feed on fruit and small berries, including poison ivy berries. They will come to feeders for sunflower seeds, suet, cornbread, cracked walnuts, peanuts, and doughnuts.

Habits: They frequently join mixed-species foraging flocks in fall and winter and are often seen in the company of chickadees, titmice, nuthatches, and kinglets.

Hairy Woodpecker
Picoides villosus

Hairy Woodpeckers look like larger versions of Downy Woodpeckers (see page 112). Since they are only 2 inches larger, however, the best way to distinguish them is by the length of their bills: Downy Woodpeckers have short, stubby bills, while Hairy Woodpeckers have bills that are as long as the depth of their heads. Also, Downy Woodpeckers have dark spots in their white outer tail feathers—Hairy Woodpeckers do not.

Ron Austing

Although Hairy Woodpeckers do not frequent feeders, you can still attract them by offering suet and peanut-butter suet mixes. Also leave or "plant" some dead snags in your backyard to provide roosting sites.

Identification Flashes and Distinguishing Features:

Look for their larger bills to help distinguish them from the similar but smaller Downy Woodpeckers.

Size: 9¼ inches (24 centimeters)

Color: Both males and females have black upperparts, tails, and wings with white bars and dots; they have white underparts, backs, and outer tail feathers. Both males and females have white faces with black ear patches and crowns; males have a red patch on the back of their heads.

Voice: They make sharp, metallic *peek* sounds that are higher in pitch than similar Downy Woodpecker sounds. They also make descending, loud kingfisher rattles and drumming, rolling tattoo sounds.

Range: They are permanent residents throughout the Southeast.

Habitat: They frequent deciduous and pine forests, parks, orchards, and woodlots. Both parents excavate a nesting cavity with a 1½-inch opening in a dead limb on a dead or dying tree.

Eggs: They lay 3–6 pure white eggs; 1 brood per breeding season. Both parents incubate the eggs—the female during the day, the male during the night; incubation takes about 20 days; It is not known how old the fledglings are when they leave the nest.

Food: More than 75 percent of their diet is insects, especially pine borers and spruce bark beetles; they also eat ants, millipedes, spiders, and stag beetles. Occasionally they feed on berries, nuts, and sap at sapsucker feeding-wells. They will come to feeders for suet and suet mixes, sunflower seeds, peanut butter, nut meats, cheese, and apples.

Habits: They appear to stay paired throughout the year and remain in the same area. These noisy woodpeckers regularly call to their mates while foraging. They are the most commonly observed woodpecker in high-elevation spruce and fir forests in eastern Tennessee, western North Carolina, and northern Georgia.

Northern (Yellow-shafted) Flicker

Colaptes auratus

They are the only brown woodpeckers that live in the Southeast. Like most woodpeckers, they seek drumming perches in the spring that provide good sounding boards. They seem to favor aluminum guttering and tin roofs— which makes their crack-of-dawn drummings especially effective!

You can attract Northern Flickers by providing nesting boxes (see Habitat, below) and by filling feeders with peanut butter, suet, and suet mixes.

Ron Austing

Identification Flashes and Distinguishing Features:

The only brown woodpecker seen in the Southeast. Look for the distinctive white rump patches and yellow underwings and tail surfaces of Northern Flickers in flight.

Size: 12½–14 inches (32–35 centimeters)

Color: Both sexes have brown upperparts with darker brown barring, tan faces, gray crowns and napes, and a red bar on the back of their heads. Only males have a black malar (moustachial) stripe. They have black crescent bibs and black spotting on their underparts. Their white rump patches and yellow underwings and tail surfaces are conspicuous in flight.

Voice: They make loud *cleearrer* sounds as well as series of identical *wick-wick-wick-wick-wick* or *wick-er, wick-er, wick-er, wick-er* sounds that, unlike the Pileated Woodpecker's sounds, don't change in pitch, loudness, or cadence.

Range: They are permanent residents throughout the Southeast.

Habitat: They frequent open areas, including lawns, farm clearings, roadsides, and open woodlots. Both parents excavate a nesting cavity in a living tree, dead snag, utility pole, or fence post. They sometimes use a nesting cavity from previous year and will accept boxes built from 1½-inch cedar boards (4½ x 7½ x 24 inches with a 2¼-inch hole cut 3 inches below the top) mounted at least 4 feet above the ground and filled with sawdust, which allows the birds to "excavate" their cavity.

Eggs: They lay 3–10 white eggs; 1 brood per breeding season. Both parents incubate the eggs—the female during the day, the male during the night; incubation takes 11–12 days. Fledglings leave nest 25–28 days after hatching.

Food: About half of their diet is ants; they also feed on beetles, caterpillars, grubs, and wasps. Fruit and small berries make up about 25 percent of diet. They will come to feeders for peanut butter, suet, and suet mixes.

Habits: They are usually seen either in the undulating flight that is typical of most woodpeckers or on the ground foraging for ants, one of their favorite foods. They give conspicuous vocal and bowing displays in spring as part of their courtship behavior.

Pileated Woodpecker
Dryocopus pileatus

These crow-size birds are the largest woodpeckers commonly seen in North America; only the Ivory-billed Woodpecker is larger, and it is probably extinct. The Pileated Woodpecker's loud, jungle-birdlike calls, large size, and the loud raps it makes when drumming on trees will command your attention.

You can attract Pileated Woodpeckers to your backyard by filling feeders with sunflower seeds, cracked corn, suet, or suet mixes.

Ron Austing

Identification Flashes and Distinguishing Features:

Look for their large size and crest, which easily distinguish them from other woodpeckers.

Size: 16–19½ inches (41–50 centimeters)

Color: Both males and females have mostly black bodies with white chins and throats; white stripes extend from their faces along their necks and sides into the pit of their wings. Males have red mustaches and crowns, including their crests. Females have black mustaches and foreheads and red-crested crowns.

Voice: They make loud, flickerlike *yucka-yucka-yucka* and *cuk-cuk-cuk-cuk* and *wick-wick-wick-wick* sounds that, unlike the sound of flickers, change in pitch, loudness, and cadence.

Range: They are permanent residents throughout the Southeast.

Habitat: They prefer mature woodlots and riverbottom hardwoods, mature pine stands, cypress swamps, and open areas bordering woodlands. Most often choose dead trees or dead stubs of living trees. Each year they excavate a new nest cavity with a 3½-inch oval to triangular entrance hole.

Eggs: They lay 3–8 oval to elliptical white eggs; 1 brood per breeding season. Both parents incubate the eggs—the female during the day, the male during the night; incubation takes 18 days. Fledglings leave nest about 30 days after hatching.

Food: Their favorite food is Carpenter Ants, which they dig out of the deep heartwood of trees. They also eat other wood-boring beetle larvae and other insects. They feed on fruit, berries, and seeds (wild grapes, dogwood, poison ivy, sour gum, cherries, sumac, acorns, and beechnuts). They sometimes come to feeders for sunflower seeds, cracked corn, suet, and suet mixes made with cornmeal and nuts.

Habits: These shy, retiring birds are more often heard—by their loud rappings on trees—than seen. They forage on the ground as well as on fallen timber, logs, and stumps in deep woodlots. Pairs often frequent the same woodlots for years, nesting and roosting near nests used in previous years.

Eastern Phoebe

Sayornis phoebe

Ron Austing

These tail-wagging birds are the hardiest of the eastern flycatchers, and they winter much farther north than any of their other family members. Eastern Phoebes have adapted well to nesting on manmade structures and are frequently seen near homes and farmsteads where flying insects and nesting ledges are plentiful.

You can attract Eastern Phoebes by providing nesting ledges (see Habitat, below) and water. They especially like moving or dripping water.

Identification Flashes and Distinguishing Features:

Eastern Phoebes wag their tails from side to side and up and down, a habit that distinguishes them from other flycatchers. Also, they are the only flycatchers that winter in the Southeast.

Size: 7 inches (18 centimeters)

Color: Both males and females have brownish-gray upperparts, with the darkest feathers on their heads, wings, and tails; whitish underparts with an olive to yellowish wash on their breasts and sides; and dark mandibles.

Voice: They sing distinctive raspy *FEE-bee* songs. In spring and early summer they frequently give sharp *chip* calls.

Range: They are permanent residents in the Southeast in areas north of Florida and the Gulf and Atlantic Coastal Plains, although their numbers drop in winter as many migrate south. Phoebes that remain in northern areas may starve during harsh winters.

Habitat: Historically they nested on ledges in rock walls; now they nest on a wide variety of manmade structures, including bridges and culverts, window shutters, eaves, rafters, and doorsills. You can attract them by mounting (with contact cement) 5-inch sections of 2 x 4 lumber to the sides of buildings 10–12 inches below the roof overhang. Although the female does most of the work, both parents gather grasses, fibers, weeds, and mud and form a 4½-inch nesting cup. They cover the nesting cup with mosses and line it with finer grasses, hair, and feathers.

Eggs: They lay 3–6 white eggs (a few eggs in the clutch may be brownish near larger end); 2–3 broods per breeding season. The female incubates the eggs; incubation takes 14–16 days. Fledglings leave nest 15–16 days after hatching.

Food: They feed mainly on flying insects (beetles, flies, mosquitoes, ants, wasps, grasshoppers, crickets, dragonflies, and moths).

Habits: They have a telltale habit of wagging their tails. Cowbirds sometimes lay their eggs in Eastern Phoebe nests, and the phoebes will often raise the young cowbirds at the expense of their own young (see Brown-headed Cowbird, page 182).

Great Crested Flycatcher

Myiarchus crinitus

These large, colorful birds will get your attention with their loud calls. They dash from conspicuous treetop perches and take insects on the wing. They are the only eastern fly-catchers that nest in cavities; they decorate their nests with a snake skin—or cellophane, if a castoff reptile skin isn't available.

You can attract them to your backyard by leaving or planting dead snags or providing nesting boxes (see Habitat, below). They will feed on available insects and berries.

Ron Austing

Identification Flashes and Distinguishing Features:

Look for their bright rufous-red tails, gray throats and upper breasts, and yellow underparts. Also look for their short, bushy crests. Listen for their loud calls.

Size: 8½ inches (21 centimeters)

Color: Both males and females have olive-brown upperparts, yellow underparts, gray throats and breasts, cinnamon-brown wings, bright rufous-red tails, and short, bushy crests.

Voice: They make loud *wheeeep!* or *creeeep!* whistles and sometimes combine notes into *wheep, wheep, wheep, preeeep!* calls.

Range: They are summer residents across the Southeast and winter visitors in South Florida.

Habitat: They frequent woodlots, old orchards, wooded lake and stream borders, farmlands, and urban areas with large shade trees. Both parents build a nesting cup from twigs, leaves, mosses, hair, bark fibers, rope, string, plant fibers, rootlets, grasses, feathers, onion skins, snake skins, or cellophane. They occasionally nest in suitable boxes (6 x 8 x 10 inches with a 2-inch hole cut 7 inches above the bottom) mounted 8–20 feet above the ground in wooded areas. They fill their nesting cavities with leaves and debris.

Eggs: They lay 4–8 pinkish or yellowish-white eggs blotched, streaked, and dotted with brown and purple; 1 brood per breeding season. The female incubates the eggs; incubation takes 13–15 days. Fledgings leave the nest 12–18 days after hatching.

Food: They feed primarily on large insects taken in flight or gleaned from the ground or tree crevices (dragonflies, moths, bees, wasps, beetles, grasshoppers, crickets, katydids, spiders, and caterpillars). They also eat berries, cherries, and grapes.

Habits: They usually perch high in trees and make swift, hawking feeding sallies, often returning to the same conspicuous perch. Sometimes they feed in the lower canopy or close to the ground. The territorial males engage in aerial combat, often tangling claws and pulling out their opponents' feathers.

Purple Martin

Progne subis

Purple Martins, the largest swallows in the Southeast, are familiar favorites and widely beloved for their insect-eating habits, social behavior, and pleasing songs.

You can attract Purple Martins to your backyard by providing nesting boxes and gourds (see Habitat, below), and you can establish nesting colonies that will return

Ron Austing

annually. You may have to discourage House Sparrows and European Starlings from nesting in the boxes or gourds before the martins arrive in the spring.

Identification Flashes and Distinguishing Features:

Look for their notched tails. From a distance, male Purple Martins appear to be a solid dark color.

Size: 8 inches (20 centimeters)

Color: Males appear all black at a distance, but they show dark, glossy purplish-black plumage in bright light. Females and juveniles have dark bluish-brown and gray upperparts, including their chins, throats, and breasts. They have whitish bellies and lower breasts. Both males and females have moderately forked tails.

Voice: During flight they make a loud, rich chirruping song of low-pitched, liquid, guttural notes. Males often sing at night.

Range: They are breeding summer residents across the Southeast. They winter in the Amazon River Valley of Brazil.

Habitat: They prefer river valleys, lake shores, coastal areas, farm-lands, and grasslands. Historically they nested in natural and abandoned woodpecker holes in trees, on cliffs, among rocks, and in gourds erected for them by Indians in the Southeast. Many of them now live in colonies in gourds and nesting boxes (6 x 6 inches inside with a 2½-inch entrance hole). Both parents build nest from grasses, twigs, bark, string, rags, paper, and leaves; they line nesting cups with finer grasses and leaves and sometimes form a mud rim at the entrance.

Eggs: They lay 3–8 pure white eggs; 1–2 broods per breeding season. The female incubates the eggs, but the male guards the nest whenever she leaves; incubation takes 15–16 days. Fledglings leave the nest 26–31 days after hatching.

Food: They feed primarily on insects (beetles, moths, butterflies, horseflies, mosquitoes, grasshoppers, leafhoppers, and dragonflies). They will come for broken chicken eggshells placed on the ground.

Habits: They take insects in flight, flycatcher style; they also forage while walking on the ground. One of the most domesticated wild birds, they have almost completely abandoned their original natural nesting sites for manmade homes. They nest in large active colonies in open areas, usually near water.

Barn Swallow

Hirundo rustica

Barn Swallows have been well-known backyard birds, especially on farmsteads, since colonial times. They are the familiar swallows we see flying low over agricultural fields and in and out of barns, where they nest on beams in small colonies.

Barn Swallows will come to your backyard if you have an open building with exposed interior beams or rafters or overhangs with suitable ledges/shelves for nesting.

Ron Austing

Identification Flashes and Distinguishing Features:

Look for the deeply forked tail that distinguishes Barn Swallows from all other North American swallows. Also look for the large white "flash" spots near the base of their tails.

Size: 6¾ inches (17 centimeters)

Color: Males and females look alike, but the males are often richer in color. They have metallic blue upperparts, reddish foreheads and throats, and buffy to white underparts. Their tails, which are the most deeply forked of all North American swallows, have large white spots near the base.

Voice: They constantly twitter, making bubbly liquidlike *wit-wit-wit* notes.

Range: Currently they are summer residents and breeding birds north of Florida and the coastal plains, but they are expanding their range. They winter in South America.

Habitat: They prefer open areas. Historically they nested on cliffs and in cave entrances and rock niches; now they nest primarily in and on manmade structures, including barns, bridges, dams, wharves, docks, and porches. They nest in pairs, either singly or in colonies of 50 or more pairs. Both parents build an open nesting cup by plastering mud and straw to a ledge. They line their nests with fine grasses and usually with feathers.

Eggs: They lay 4–6 white eggs with brown spots and dots; 1–2 broods per breeding season. Both parents incubate the eggs during the day, and female incubates them at night; incubation takes 13–17 days. Fledglings leave the nest 18–23 days after hatching, but they may return for several nights before leaving it for good.

Food: They feed primarily on insects.

Habits: They bathe and drink by skimming standing water. In spring and summer they can often be seen following farm machinery and catching insects in swift continuous flights over open ground. Some individual Barn Swallows may migrate the greatest distance of any New World land birds, traveling more than 7,000 miles twice annually from their wintering grounds in Argentina to their breeding sites in Alaska.

Tree Swallow
Tachycineta bicolor

They are the only swallows that normally winter in the Southeast, and thousands of them can be seen along the Gulf Coastal Plains and across Florida. They effectively reduce flying-insect populations. They are the first swallows to arrive in northern areas in the spring, and when insects are not readily available, they feed on berries and seeds.

You can easily attract Tree Swallows by providing nesting boxes (see Habitat, below).

Ron Austing

Identification Flashes and Distinguishing Features:

Look for their slightly notched tails, white underparts, and metallic-green upperparts.

Size: 5¾ inches (15 centimeters)

Color: Adults have glossy greenish-black or blue-black upperparts; females are paler than males and have a brown wash on their heads and backs. Their underparts, including their chins and the sides of their faces below their eyes, are snowy white. Juveniles have brownish-gray upperparts and white underparts, sometimes with a grayish-brown breast band.

Voice: They often make a sweet liquid chatter of rapidly repeated silip notes while in flight.

Range: Currently they are summer residents and breeding birds throughout the Mississippi River Alluvial Plain and its tributaries eastward across Tennessee into the Southern Blue Ridge area, but they are expanding their breeding range. They winter in the Atlantic and Gulf Coastal Plains and Florida.

Habitat: They frequent wooded areas near water. As secondary-cavity nesters, they nest in natural cavities, abandoned woodpecker holes, holes in buildings, and nesting boxes (5½ x 4 x 6 inches with a 1½-inch hole cut 1½ inches from the top) mounted 4–6 feet off the ground on posts spaced 100 yards apart in open areas near water. They nest in single pairs or loose colonies. Females build nests from grass and straw and line them with feathers.

Eggs: They lay 4–6 white eggs; 1 brood per breeding season. The female incubates the eggs; incubation takes 13–16 days. Fledglings leave the nest 16–24 days after hatching.

Food: They feed primarily on insects taken in flight (flies, wasps, beetles, spiders, ants, grasshoppers, and crickets). They also land on beaches and feed on the small crustaceans known as "beach fleas." In cold weather they eat small seeds (smartweed, bulrush, sedges, and bayberry fruit).

Habits: They readily accept nesting boxes scattered in open areas near water. Fall migrating flocks may number into the thousands.

Fred J. Alsop III

Blue Jay
Cyanocitta cristata

Although almost everyone recognizes these highly intelligent, colorful birds, not everyone welcomes them. They are noisy, generally have their way at feeders, and occasionally take young birds from other birds' nests—all of which give them a generally undeserved bad reputation. On the plus side, Blue Jays are often the first to sound the alarm note that sends other birds diving for cover.

You can attract them by providing water and offering sunflower seeds, corn, nuts, suet, or suet mixes in platform, hopper, and hanging feeders.

Fred J. Alsop III

Ron Austing

Identification Flashes and Distinguishing Features:

They are the only crested blue-and-white birds in the Southeast.

Size: 11 inches (28 centimeters)

Color: They have bright-blue upperparts, crests, and napes; white underparts and faces, with a black necklace around their necks; black bars and white patches on wings; black bars on their tails; and white tips on all but their center tail feathers.

Voice: They make loud *jay, jay, jay, thief, thief, thief,* and double-noted *tull-ull* calls that sound like a squeaking pump handle. They also make loud hawklike calls and softer vocalizations.

Range: They are permanent residents across the Southeast.

Habitat: Historically they preferred large woodlands but have adapted well to urbanization and fragmentation of forests. They nest in deciduous or conifer trees on a large branch or where a limb joins the trunk. Both parents build bulky nest from grasses, twigs, string, leaves, mosses, lichens, rags, paper, and other available natural and manmade materials. They line nesting cups with softer, finer materials.

Eggs: They lay 3–6 olive, buff, or greenish-bluish gray eggs that have gray or brown dots and spots; 2–3 broods per breeding season. The female incubates the eggs; incubation takes 16–18 days. Fledglings leave the nest 17–21 days after hatching.

Food: They eat an omnivorous diet that is 75 percent vegetable (large seeds, small berries, and nuts from a variety of plants); they prefer acorns, beechnuts, corn, and palmetto seeds. They also eat insects, worms, snails, frogs, salamanders, small fish, small rodents, small bats, and occasionally eggs and young of smaller birds. They will come to feeders for suet, peanut butter, peanuts, or sunflower seeds

Habits: They are clever learners and can be easily tamed to take peanuts from your hand. They frequent birdbaths for drinking and bathing. They store beech and oak seeds for winter food; some of the seeds not retrieved by the birds play an important role in seed distribution and the "replanting" of woodlands.

American Crow

Corvus brachyrhynchos

Even though American Crows are smaller than ravens, they are the largest crows in North America. They are also some of the best known and most easily recognized

birds, and "crow-size" has become a useful reference in describing other birds. They live in many different habitats and have made positive adjustments to increased human populations.

You can attract crows by providing water and offering corn, sunflower seeds, peanuts, or suet either on the ground or in feeders.

Ron Austing

Identification Flashes and Distinguishing Features:

They are the only large, all-black birds seen in the Southeast except for waterbirds along the coasts and in the Mississippi River floodplain. Look for their distinctive flight that has deep, steady wingbeats and resembles rowing motions.

Size: 17½–19 inches (45–48 centimeters)

Color: They have completely black bodies. The glossy metallic black feathers on their backs and heads shimmer with sheens of deep purple, green, and blue.

Voice: Their nasal *caw, caw, caw* is one of the most-recognized wild bird sounds. They also produce more melodic notes as well as imitations of human and other animal sounds.

Range: They are permanent residents across the Southeast.

Habitat: They frequent deciduous or conifer trees. Both parents build bulky, 2-foot nesting cup in a tree crotch or the fork of a large limb. They use sticks to make their nest and line it with bark, leaves, rootlets, vines, grass, feathers, hair, fur, and other available natural and manmade materials.

Eggs: They lay 3–8 blue-gray or green eggs spotted with browns and grays, sometimes on a reddish background; 1–2 broods per breeding season. Both parents incubate the eggs; incubation takes 18 days. Fledglings leave nest 28–35 days after hatching.

Food: They eat a wide variety of vegetable and animal fare (cultivated fruit, corn and other cultivated grains, grasshoppers and other large insects, crustaceans, frogs, salamanders, small reptiles, small mammals, carrion, earthworms, and the eggs and young of other birds). They also eat crabs and sea urchins, which they carry aloft and drop from considerable heights to break open.

Habits: In winter they sometimes roost in large flocks that number into the thousands. Their distinctive flight has deep, steady wingbeats that resemble the motions of rowing a boat.

Fish Crow
Corvus ossifragus

Fish Crows, which look like small American Crows (see page 124), frequent tidewater marshes, beaches, mudflats, and inland reaches of slow, meandering rivers. They are often found in small flocks and family groups, but wintering flocks may number into the thousands.

You can attract them to your backyard by filling feeders with suet or peanut butter-suet mixes and by offering sunflower seeds either on the ground or on platform feeders. They will nest and perch in available large trees.

Fred J. Alsop III

Identification Flashes and Distinguishing Features:

Their smaller size, narrower bills, and more pointed wings distinguish them from American Crows. Listen for their distinctive nasal, froglike, falsetto calls.

Size: 15½ inches (39 centimeters)

Color: They have all-black bodies, including bills, legs, and feet.

Voice: They make nasal, froglike, falsetto *ah-ah, ah-ah, ah-uk* calls.

Range: They are permanent residents from the Mississippi River Alluvial Plain to northwest Tennessee, the East Gulf Coastal Plain, Florida, and the South Atlantic and Mid-Atlantic Coastal Plains. Some of them move inland during winter months.

Habitat: They frequent coastal, tidewater, and freshwater marshes, swamps, mudflats, beaches, lakes, and rivers. They nest in small loose colonies in tree groves, each pair nesting in a separate tree. Both sexes build their nest using sticks, twigs, and bark fibers; they line the finished nest with pine needles, bark strips, grasses, roots, vines, hair, and feathers.

Eggs: They lay 4–6 bluish, greenish, or grayish-green eggs liberally blotched and spotted with brown and gray; 1 brood per breeding season. Both parents incubate the eggs; incubation takes 16–18 days. Fledglings leave the nest 21 days after hatching.

Food: They eat primarily animal fare taken in or near water (shrimp, crabs, crayfish, tubeworms, and carrion). Occasionally they take the eggs of waterbirds; they also take turtle eggs and young. They pick grasshoppers, ants, and ticks off the backs of cattle. They occasionally feed on apples, corn, and berries and seeds (cedar, holly, dogwood, palmetto, magnolia, and other trees and shrubs).

Habits: These social, gregarious crows almost never travel or forage singly. They soar and hover more frequently than American Crows do.

Carolina Chickadee

Poecilen (Parus) carolinensis

Many people mistakenly think the Carolina Chickadees they see at their feeders are the larger Black-capped Chickadees. The only place in the Southeast where Black-capped Chickadees are found at any time of the year is the Southern Blue Ridge mountains in eastern Tennessee and western North Carolina.

You can attract Carolina Chickadees to your backyard by providing suitable nesting boxes (see Habitat, below) and by filling feeders with sunflower or thistle seeds, suet, or suet mixes.

Ron Austing

Ron Austing

Ron Austing

Identification Flashes and Distinguishing Features:

Look for their distinctive white faces and black caps and bibs. Where you see them will help you distinguish Carolina Chickadees from Black-capped Chickadees, which are seen only in the Southern Blue Ridge mountains.

Size: 4¾ inches (12 centimeters)

Color: They have ashy-gray upperparts; pale whitish-gray underparts with buffy flanks; white faces; and black caps and bibs.

Voice: Males whistle a clear *fee-bee, fee-bay* during breeding season. Males and females sing familiar *chick-a-dee-dee-dee* year-round. When disturbed, incubating birds hiss like a snake.

Range: They are permanent residents and breeding birds everywhere in the Southeast except Tropical Florida and above 4,000 feet in the Southern Blue Ridge mountains.

Habitat: They frequent coniferous, deciduous, and mixed-hardwood woodlots. As secondary-cavity nesters, they nest in natural tree cavities, abandoned woodpecker holes, fence posts, and suitable nesting boxes (4 x 4 x 8 inches with a 1⅛-inch hole cut 2 inches below the top) mounted 5–15 feet above the ground on posts or in trees. They sometimes excavate nesting cavites in dead wood when the wood is soft enough, and they occasionally build nests in the iron pipe crosstrees of rural clotheslines. Their nests have a thick foundation of mosses and are lined with hair, thin grasses, and plant down.

Eggs: They lay 3–8 white eggs rather evenly dotted with reddish brown; 1 brood per breeding season. Both parents incubate the eggs; incubation takes 11–13 days. Fledglings leave the nest 12–14 days after hatching.

Food: In summer they primarily eat moths and caterpillars. They also eat seeds and small berries. They will come to feeders for black oil sunflower seeds, thistle seeds, or suet.

Habits: Pairs stay together for several years. They are often seen in mixed-species feeding flocks with Downy Woodpeckers, nuthatches, Tufted Titmice, wrens, kinglets, and warblers. They take one sunflower seed at a time, fly to a perch, hold down the seed with their feet, and peck open the seed coat.

Ron Austing

Tufted Titmouse

Baeolophus (Parus) bicolor

These perky little gray birds are easily recognized by their rusty flanks, button-black eyes, and crested heads. You can easily draw titmice (and chickadees) to you by making loud, squeaking noises by kissing the back of your hand or imitating Eastern Screech-Owl calls. When they sound the alarm, other birds will come to the scene.

You can attract Tufted Titmice by providing water and nesting boxes (see Habitat, page 129) and by offering sunflower seeds or suet.

Ron Austing

Identification Flashes and Distinguishing Features:

Look for their gray bodies, rusty flanks, button-black eyes, and crested heads.

Size: 6½ inches (17 centimeters)

Color: They have grayish upperparts, including gray crests; black foreheads; and whitish to pale-gray underparts, with a rusty wash on their sides and flanks.

Voice: They make loud, clear *peter, peter, peter* whistles and sometimes *peto, peto, peto* sounds.

Range: They are permanent residents throughout the Southeast except Tropical Florida.

Habitat: They prefer woodland habitats, especially bottomland hardwoods and low-elevation mixed-hardwood and hardwood forests; they also reside in wooded residential areas. As secondary-cavity nesters, they nest in natural cavities, abandoned woodpecker holes, fence posts, and suitable nesting boxes (4 x 4 x 8 inches with a 1⅜ hole cut 2 inches below the top) mounted 5–15 feet above the ground in trees or on poles in or near wooded areas. They make their nests from mosses, leaves, bark fibers, plant down, shed snake skin, hair (sometimes plucked from animals and people), and other natural materials.

Eggs: They lay 4–8 white eggs that have dark brown dots and spots clustered at the large end; 1–2 broods per breeding season. The female incubates the eggs, and the male feeds her while she is on the nest; incubation takes 13–14 days. Fledglings leave the nest 17–18 days after hatching.

Food: In summer they eat primarily insects (caterpillars, sawfly larvae, treehoppers, ants, beetles, and wasps). They also eat small berries (poison ivy, blueberries, blackberries, wild cherries, and serviceberries) and large seeds (acorns, beechnuts, tulip poplar, sunflower, and sumac). They will come to feeders for sunflower seeds, peanuts, nuts, suet, and suet mixes.

Habits: They hold large seeds between their feet and hack them open with their beaks. In winter they often travel in mixed-species foraging flocks with chickadees, nuthatches, kinglets, Downy Woodpeckers, and other small birds.

Ron Austing

Red-breasted Nuthatch

Sitta canadensis

The bird's colloquial name "nuthack" has been altered through the years to "nuthatch." They live in northern coniferous forests and make erratic appearances in the Southeast during severe winters when food is scarce in the North. Red-breasted Nuthatches, like other nuthatches, do not typically migrate.

You can attract visiting Red-breasted Nuthatches by filling feeders with sunflower seeds, suet, or suet mixes.

Ron Austing

Identification Flashes and Distinguishing Features:

Their ability to walk down trees headfirst distinguishes nuthatches from all other birds. Look for the distinctive reddish underparts and black eye lines on Red-breasted Nuthatches. Unless you live in the Southern Blue Ridge area, you probably will see them only during winter months.

Size: 4½ inches (11 centimeters)

Color: Males and females look alike, but females have paler underparts and heads. Their backs, wings, and tails are bluish-gray; their underparts are rusty red. They have white faces with a black line "through" their eyes and black caps.

Voice: They make *waa-waa-waa-waa-waa* songs that sounds like a toy tin horn. They also make *ank, ank, ank* calls.

Range: They are breeding birds in the Southern Blue Ridge forests of eastern Tennessee and western North Carolina. They are winter visitors as far south as the Florida peninsula.

Habitat: They prefer conifers, particularly spruce, pine, and hemlock. They usually dig holes in the soft wood of rotting tree stubs; they sometimes use natural cavities, abandoned woodpecker holes, or nesting boxes (4 x 4 x 8 inches with a 1¼-inch hole cut 2 inches below the top) mounted 10–20 feet above the ground in wooded areas. They build nests from mosses, grasses, rootlets, and shredded bark fibers. They gather pitch from conifers and smear it around the entrance holes.

Eggs: They lay 4–7 white eggs peppered with red-brown dots or spots; 1 brood per breeding season. Both parents incubate the eggs; incubation takes about 12 days. Fledglings leave the nest 18–21 days after hatching.

Food: They feed primarily on seeds, particularly conifer seeds. In summer they eat some insects (spruce budworm, beetles, wasps, and caterpillars). They will come to feeders for sunflower seeds, hulled walnuts, or suet.

Habits: When foraging they walk down trees headfirst. They wedge large seeds and nuts into crevices in tree bark and then hack open the seed coats. They often store seeds for winter food.

White-breasted Nuthatch

Sitta carolinensis

White-breasted Nuthatches are the largest North American nuthatches. They remain together in pairs all year and roam over large winter territories (25 to 50 acres). They are often seen walking headfirst down trees. Their colloquial name "nuthack" has been altered through the years to "nuthatch."

You can attract nuthatches to your backyard by providing suitable nesting boxes (see Habitat, below) and by filling feeders with sunflower seeds or suet and suet mixes.

Ron Austing

Identification Flashes and Distinguishing Features:

Their ability to walk down trees headfirst distinguishes nuthatches from all other birds. Look for their distinctive, handsome blue-gray upperparts and white underparts.

Size: 5¾ inches (15 centimeters)

Color: Males and females look alike, but females may have paler crowns. They have blue-gray upperparts, black caps and napes, white faces, white underparts, white tail patches, and a rusty wash on their flanks and undertail coverts.

Voice: They make nasal *yank* sounds. They also sing 6–8 *yank* running notes that sound a bit like an old car trying to start.

Range: They are permanent residents throughout the Southeast except the Florida peninsula.

Habitat: They prefer deciduous forests and woodlots below 3,500 feet; they also frequent wooded urban areas. As secondary-cavity nesters, they nest in natural cavities, abandoned woodpecker holes, and sometimes in nesting boxes (4 x 4 x 8 inches with a 1¼-inch hole cut 2 inches below the top) mounted 10–20 feet above the ground in wooded areas. They line their nests with mosses, rootlets, bark shreds, grasses, fur, feathers, and hair.

Eggs: They lay 5–10 white eggs peppered with spots or dots of reddish-brown, gray, and purple; 1 brood per breeding season. Both parents incubate the eggs; incubation takes about 12 days. Fledglings leave the nest about 14 days after hatching.

Food: In spring and summer they feed primarily on insects. Fall and winter fare includes seeds, nuts, and berries. They will come to feeders for sunflower seeds, cracked nuts, peanuts, and suet.

Habits: They take one seed at a time and either store it or wedge it into a crack so they can hack it open. In winter they join mixed-species foraging flocks. They "threaten" other birds by partially spreading their wings and tails and making half-turns, with their necks and heads extended. Pairs mate for life, and both parents "bill sweep" in or near their nest, swinging their upper bodies back and forth while holding insects in their beaks for their young.

Brown-headed Nuthatch

Sitta pusilla

Traditionally birds of the pine forests of the South, Brown-headed Nuthatches are now permanent residents in many parts of the Southeast. They are the smallest of the eastern nuthatches and are often seen in noisy family groups before and after breeding season.

You can attract Brown-headed Nuthatches to your backyard by leaving or "planting" dead snags or providing suitable nesting boxes (see Habitat, below). They will also come to feeders filled with sunflower seeds or suet.

A. Murphy/Vireo

Identification Flashes and Distinguishing Features:

Their ability to walk down a tree trunk headfirst distinguishes nuthatches from other birds. Also look for their small size, bluish-gray upperparts, and brown heads.

Size: 4½ inches (11 centimeters)

Color: Both males and females have bluish-gray backs, wings, and tails; white underparts and sides of faces below eyes; brown to brownish gray caps, napes, and faces above eyes; and a white spot at the base of their napes.

Voice: They make a *pit, pit, pit* sound as well as a *weebee, weebee, weebee* that sounds a bit like a rubber bathtub duck.

Range: They are permanent residents on the Piedmont and coastal plains of the Southeast; they do not live in Tropical Florida. They are expanding their range northward.

Habitat: They frequent open woodlands of pine, scrub oak, and cypress trees as well as pine stands, clearings, and burned-over tracts. Both parents excavate a nesting cavity in the soft wood of decaying pine stubs or stumps. They sometimes nest in abandoned woodpecker holes, fence posts, and nesting boxes (4 x 4 x 8 inches with a 1⅛ hole cut 2 inches below the top) mounted 6–10 feet above the ground in wooded areas. They line nests with grasses, bark chips, weed stems, cotton, feathers, pine seed husks, and other soft natural materials.

Eggs: They lay 3–9 white eggs that are heavily dotted and splotched with reddish brown; 1 brood per breeding season. Both parents incubate the eggs; incubation takes about 14 days. Fledglings leave the nest cavity about 18 days after hatching.

Food: They feed on a variety of insects gleaned from tree trunks and limbs. They also feed on the seeds of pine trees. Occasionally they come to feeders filled with sunflower seeds and suet.

Habits: They often work out to the tips of limbs and hang upside down, chickadee fashion, as they feed on insects. Except for the breeding season, they live in family groups and are often seen with chickadees, titmice, warblers, kinglets, and creepers. They tend to be very vocal.

Brown Creeper
Certhia americana

For the most part, Brown Creepers are solitary birds. They are often seen foraging on the trunks and larger limbs of trees. They habitually hop upward, like woodpeckers but in a spiral—rather than a straight line—around the trunk. When they near the top of the tree, they fly downward to a spot at the base of a nearby tree and start their upward spiral once more.

You can attract Brown Creepers to your backyard by filling feeders with suet, peanut butter-suet mixes, or chopped peanuts.

Fred J. Alsop III

Identification Flashes and Distinguishing Features:

Look for their small size, distinctive down-curved bill, streaked brown plummage, and upward spiraling foraging behavior.

Size: 5¼ inches (13 centimeters)

Color: Both males and females have white underparts and white stripes over their eyes. The camouflaged streaks and spots of white and black on brown on their upperparts match tree bark. They have long, slender down-curved bills.

Voice: They make long *tsss* or *seee* calls as well as series of high-pitched notes that sound like shortened Winter Wren songs.

Range: They are winter visitors across the Southeast and can be found wherever there are large trees. They breed in the northern hardwood and spruce-fir forests of the Southern Blue Ridge area of eastern Tennessee and western North Carolina.

Habitat: They usually build their nests under slabs of dead bark still attached to living or dead trees; they sometimes build nests in natural cavities or abandoned woodpecker holes. They make hammock-shaped nests from grasses, bark strips, leaves, and twigs. They line their nests with finer grasses, mosses, and sometimes feathers.

Eggs: They lay 4–8 white eggs that are spotted with reddish brown; 1 brood per breeding season. Both parents incubate the eggs; incubation takes 14–15 days. Fledglings leave the nest 13–14 days after hatching.

Food: They eat primarily insects (insect larvae, moths, pupae, weevils, caterpillars, spiders, and others). They feed on some nuts and seeds and will come to feeders for chopped peanuts, suet, or suet mixes.

Habits: They spiral upward on trees when they forage. In winter they can be seen in mixed-species feeding flocks with chickadees, titmice, and nuthatches. At night they often sleep by clinging vertically to the bark of a tree with their long, sharp claws.

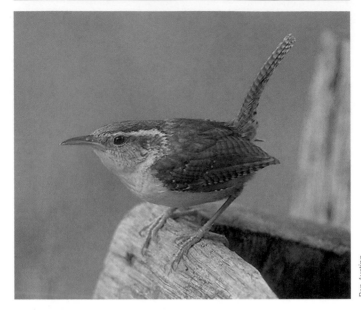

Ron Austing

Carolina Wren

Thryothorus ludovicianus

Carolina Wrens, the largest wrens in eastern North America, are our familiar energetic backyard songsters. These active wrens often carry their tails at jaunty angles over their backs. They are creatures of thickets, where they explore the tangles' dark crevices, holes, and tunnels for insects. Troglodytidae, the scientific name for the wren family, means "cave dweller" and refers to the dark places where wrens forage as well as to the cavities or domed nests they build.

You can attract Carolina Wrens to your backyard by planting dense shrubbery, providing birdbaths and other sources of water, and by filling feeders with suet or peanut butter-suet mixes.

Ron Austing

Ron Austing

Identification Flashes and Distinguishing Features:

Their relatively large size, buffy underparts, white lines over their eyes, and jauntily held tails readily distinguish Carolina Wrens from other birds.

Size: 5½ inches (14 centimeters)

Color: Both males and females have reddish-brown upperparts with white throats and eye stripes; their underparts are buffy. They have slender, down-curved bills.

Voice: They make loud, ringing *teakettle, teakettle, teakettle* or shorter *sweetheart, sweetheart, sweetheart* songs and long, drawn-out *chirrrrrrrrrrrr* calls.

Range: They are permanent residents throughout the Southeast. They suffer heavy population drops in severe winters.

Habitat: They frequent woodlots, thickets, hammocks, swamps, and residential areas. They build nests in almost any available cavity, including old woodpecker holes and holes in fence posts, stonewalls, tree stumps, and buildings as well as nesting boxes, pails, pockets of hanging cloths, mailboxes, open cans, open bags, and hanging baskets. Both parents build a domed nest of leaves, grasses, sticks, twigs, mosses, weed stalks, feathers, debris, and occasionally snake skins. They line their nest with finer materials.

Eggs: They lay 3–8 white to pale-pink eggs that may be heavily dotted or blotched with dark brown; 2 broods per breeding season. The female incubates the eggs; incubation takes about 14 days. Fledgings leave the nest 13–14 days after hatching.

Food: They eat primarily insects (spiders, beetles, stinkbugs, leafhoppers, moths, caterpillars, roaches, grasshoppers, sow bugs, millipedes, snails, and treefrogs). They also eat small lizards. They will come to feeders for suet and suet mixes.

Habits: They sing at all times of day throughout the year. They are the most commonly seen wrens in the Southeast.

House Wren
Troglodytes aedon

Persistent singers and noisy scolders, male House Wrens busy themselves building "dummy" nests in every available suitable cavity before the females arrive in the spring. The females make the final choice of the one nesting site for the pair. House Wrens are so territorial that they may destroy nests and kill the eggs and young of other birds, including other House Wrens.

You can attract House Wrens to your backyard by providing suitable nesting boxes (see Habitat, page 137) and offering suet or peanut butter-suet mixes.

Ron Austing

Ron Austing

Identification Flashes and Distinguishing Features:

Their lack of distinguishing features makes House Wrens easy to identify.

Size: 4¾ inches (12 centimeters)

Color: The plainest members of the wren family, both male and female House Wrens have brownish-gray upperparts, grayish-buff underparts, and indistinct pale stripes over their eyes. Their tails, wings, and flanks have black bars.

Voice: They produce a bubbling, energetic *tsi-tsi-tsi-tsi-oodle-oodle-oodle* song.

Range: They are summer residents and breeding birds north of the coastal plains and southern Piedmont; they currently nest throughout Tennessee and North Carolina but are expanding their breeding range southward. They winter on the coastal plains and in Florida.

Habitat: They prefer deciduous low woody vegetation, thickets, tangles, brush piles, and areas around human habitation. They nest in natural cavities in trees, stubs, fence posts, old woodpecker holes, and nesting boxes (4 x 4 x 6 inches with a 1-inch hole cut 2 inches from the top) mounted on posts or suspended from limbs 5–10 feet above the ground in wooded areas or gardens. The male builds the nest from sticks and twigs, and the female lines them with grasses, feathers, paper, leaves, rootlets, plant fibers, and hair.

Eggs: They lay 5–9 white eggs speckled with reddish or brown dots; 2-3 broods per breeding season. The female incubates the eggs; incubation takes 12–15 days. Fledglings leave the nest 12–18 days after hatching.

Food: They eat primarily insects (wasps, ants, beetles, moths, crickets, grasshoppers, flies, ticks, spiders, and millipedes). They also eat snails. Sometimes they will come to feeders for suet or peanut butter-suet mixes.

Habits: They are known for their persistent vocalizations and for the wide variety of places they choose as nesting sites.

Ron Austing

Golden-crowned Kinglet

Regulus satrapa

Kinglets, who are members of the family of Old World warblers, are more closely related to thrushes and gnatcatchers than to New World wood warblers. They are among the smallest of North American songbirds and glean insects from the outermost branches of trees, flicking their wings as they forage.

You can attract them to your backyard by including cedar, hemlock, and other conifer trees in your naturescape.

Ron Austing

Identification Flashes and Distinguishing Features:

Their small size, olive-green color, and the black and white stripes on their heads distinguish them from other birds. Look for the distinctive flicking of their wings while they forage.

Size: 4 inches (10 centimeters)

Color: Both males and females have olive-green upperparts and paler underparts, two yellowish-white wing bars, white stripes over their eyes, and black lines "through" their eyes. Their crowns have black borders with yellow or orange interiors; males have orange to red-orange crowns; females have yellow crowns.

Voice: They make high, thin *zeet-zeet-zeet* calls, and their songs begin with several *zeet* notes but continue with several louder staccato notes that fall in pitch.

Range: They are very localized permanent residents in the Southeast and breed only in the high-elevation forests of the Southern Blue Ridge area in eastern Tennessee and western North Carolina. They winter throughout the Southeast except Tropical Florida.

Habitat: They frequent conifer trees and usually nest in spruces. Females build their nests from mosses and lichens and line them with bark fibers, rootlets, and feathers.

Eggs: They lay 5–10 tiny white eggs spotted with browns and grays and deposited in 2 layers; 1 brood per breeding season. The female incubates the eggs; incubation takes 14–15 days. It is not known how old the fledglings are when they leave the nest.

Food: Their eat primarily insects and their eggs, including bark beetles, aphids, and scale insects. In winter months they sometimes feed on tree sap at the sapsucker feeding-wells.

Habits: They are very tame, unsuspicious, and easily approached. They nervously flick their wings as they hop from branch to branch. They sometimes make quick aerial dashes to catch flying insects. In winter months they often forage in mixed-species flocks with chickadees, titmice, nuthatches, and creepers.

Ruby-crowned Kinglet
Regulus calendula

Seen around homes in the Southeast only during spring and fall migration and as a winter visitor, Ruby-crowned Kinglets appear to be nondescript small greenish birds. However, displaying males often flash their brilliant scarlet crown patches.

You can attract Ruby-crowned Kinglets by including cedar, hemlock, and other conifer trees in your naturescape. They will feed on available insects.

Ron Austing

Identification Flashes and Distinguishing Features:

Their small size, olive-green color, white rings around large dark eyes, and scarlet crown patches of the males distinguish them from other birds. Look for the distinctive flicking of their wings while they forage.

Size: 4¼ inches (11 centimeters)

Color: Both males and females have greenish-gray upperparts and paler underparts, with a greenish-yellow wash on their bellies, flanks, and undertail coverts. They have white wing bars and bold white rings around their large dark eyes. Males have concealed red crown patches that they display only during breeding season.

Voice: They make wrenlike *jha-dit* calls as well as surprisingly loud musical songs with warbled *liberty, liberty, liberty* phrases.

Range: They migrate throughout the Southeast in spring and fall. They breed in boreal coniferous forests from the northeastern United States northward into Canada. They winter from the Piedmont and coastal plains southward through Florida.

Habitat: They prefer to nest in conifer trees, and they build deep, pensile nesting cups far out on branches. They build their nests with mosses and lichens and line them with plant fibers, rootlets, bark, fibers, fur, and feathers.

Eggs: They lay 5–11 white eggs evenly covered with fine red-brown dots (indistinguishable from Golden-crowned Kinglet's eggs); 1 brood per breeding season. The female incubates the eggs; incubation takes about 12 days. Fledglings leave the nest about 12 days after hatching.

Food: They eat primarily insects gleaned from foliage and by hawking in flight. They occasionally feed on sap at sapsucker feeding-wells. In winter they also feed on small seeds.

Habits: They nervously flick their wings as they hop. In winter they forage close to the ground in evergreens and thickets near water, often in mixed-species flocks with chickadees, titmice, nuthatches, and creepers. They sometimes make quick aerial dashes to catch flying insects.

Blue-gray Gnatcatcher
Polioptial caerulea

Ron Austing

These little birds resemble tiny mockingbirds with slender proportions and long tails that are often cocked over their backs. They actively forage near the tips of the branches and sometimes dart out for flying insects. They make high-pitched notes that sound like baby birds begging to be fed.

You can attract Blue-gray Gnatcatchers to your backyard by including a variety of trees and shrubs in your naturescape to provide nesting sites and insect-rich foraging areas.

Identification Flashes and Distinguishing Features:

Their small size and mockingbird-like appearance make them easy to identify. Look for their long, white-edged black tails.

Size: 4½ inches (11 centimeters)

Color: Both males and females have blue-gray upperparts, white underparts, black tails edged in white, and white rings around their eyes. During the breeding season, males have darker backs, black foreheads, and black lines over their eyes.

Voice: They frequently make high, thin *spee, spee, spee* calls. They sometimes softly warble the *spee* notes of their call.

Range: They are permanent residents and breeding birds in Florida and on the coastal plains. They are migrant and summer residents farther north of the coastal plains.

Habitat: They frequent parklike stands of trees, shade trees in residential areas, open woodlands, and areas of shrubby growth, especially near streams and pinelands. They often build their nests on horizontal tree forks. Both parents build large hummingbird-style nests from plant down, fibers, and catkins tied together with spider silk and covered with plant down and lichens. They line their nests with plant down, feathers, hair, plant tendrils, and other soft natural materials.

Eggs: They lay 3–6 bluish-white to pale-blue eggs speckled with small reddish-brown spots. Both parents incubate the eggs; incubation takes about 13 days. Fledglings leave the nest 10–12 days after hatching.

Food: They eat only insects.

Habits: They actively forage on outer branches for insects and also make aerial sallies to catch flying insects. They sometimes dismantle partially constructed nests (perhaps because they were disturbed during the building process) and reuse the materials to construct a new nest at a new site. They often hold their white-edged black tails over their backs, like wrens, and jerk their tails from side to side.

Eastern Bluebird

Sialia sialis

Eastern Bluebirds rank among the best-known and best-loved North American birds. Bright-blue upperparts and red-brown breasts and throats make the males hard to miss.

You can attract them by providing nesting boxes; House Sparrows and European Starlings will compete fiercely with them, but you can eliminate some of the competition by making bluebird-size boxes (see Habitat, below). They

Ron Austing

will come for water and to feeders for mealworms and commercial "bluebird mixes."

Identification Flashes and Distinguishing Features:

You will readily identify male Eastern Bluebirds by their bright-blue upperparts and reddish-brown breasts and throats. They are the only bluebirds that reside in the Southeast.

Size: 7 inches (18 centimeters)

Color: Males have bright blue upperparts, reddish-brown breasts and throats, and white bellies and and undertail coverts. Females are paler and duller than males and have pale blue-gray heads. Immature bluebirds have grayish upperparts, gray-and-white spotted underparts, and bluish tails.

Voice: They make soft, melodious *purity* or *tur-a-lly* calls and *cheer-up cheerful charlie* songs.

Range: They are permanent residents across the Southeast.

Habitat: They frequent open country, orchards, farms, gardens, and parks. They build their nests in natural cavities in trees, fence posts, old woodpecker holes, and nesting boxes (5 x 5 x 8 inches with a 1½ hole cut 2 inches from the top) mounted 5–10 feet above the ground on posts spaced 100 yards apart in open areas. Females build nests from grasses, weeds, and pine needles and line them with finer grasses, hair, and feathers.

Eggs: They lay 3–7 (1 less egg for second brood) pale-blue, blue`-white, or white unmarked eggs; 2-3 broods per breeding season. The female incubates the eggs; incubation takes 13–16 days. Fledglings leave the nest 15–20 days after hatching.

Food: They eat mostly insects taken from a low perch, and their diet includes grasshoppers, crickets, beetles, millipedes, katydids, and spiders. They also eat small reptiles, amphibians, fruit, and berries. They will come to feeders for mealworms, peanut butter-suet mixes, cornmeal mixtures, and commercial "bluebird mixes."

Habits: Thousands of bluebirds nest in boxes placed along roadsides and other sites. Most bluebirds remain on nesting grounds during winter months and use the boxes for night roosts. Sometimes they huddle with other bluebirds for warmth.

Hermit Thrush

Catharus guttatus

Ron Austing

Hermit Thrushes, the only "spot-breasted" thrushes in the Southeast during winter, frequent hardwoods and pines, especially where vines and groundcover are present. These shy birds may skulk under the shrubbery in your backyard and occasionally visit your birdbath.

You can attract Hermit Thrushes to your backyard by including berry-producing shrubs in your naturescape and providing water.

Identification Flashes and Distinguishing Features:

Their spotted breasts, rufous-red tails, and olive-brown backs distinguish Hermit Thrushes from other birds. Look for their distinctive habit of slowly raising and lowering their tails.

Size: 6 inches (17 centimeters)

Color: Both males and females have olive-brown upperparts, rufous-red tails and rumps, and white underparts with buffy-brown sides. Their breasts, upper bellies, and sides are heavily spotted with dark brown, buff, and gray, and they have white rings around their eyes.

Voice: They rarely sing on their wintering grounds until just before migrating in early spring. Their song consists of flute-like tones rising and descending in sequential patterns, each song beginning on a different pitch from the previous one. They make *chuck* or *chuck-chuck* calls.

Range: They winter throughout the Southeast and migrate at least as far north as the Southern Blue Ridge area of eastern Tennessee and western North Carolina to breed.

Habitat: They frequent coniferous and mixed hardwood-conifer forests. Females use twigs, mosses, bark strips, grasses, and ferns to build nesting cups either on the ground hidden under a small tree or near the ground in a small tree. They line their nests with rootlets, fine grasses, and conifer needles.

Eggs: They lay 3–6 pale-blue to blue-green eggs occasionally spotted lightly with brown; 1 brood per breeding season. The female incubates the eggs, and the male feeds her while she is on the nest; incubation takes 12 days. Fledgings leave the nest about 12 days after hatching.

Food: In spring and summer they eat primarily insects taken on the ground (ants, beetles, crickets, grasshoppers, caterpillars, sowbugs, spiders, and earthworms). In fall and winter they eat primarily fruit and berries (dogwood, pokeberry, blueberry, mistletoe, elderberry, serviceberry, and poison ivy).

Habits: As their name suggests, they are often shy and retiring. They slightly raise and lower their tails, especially after perching.

Wood Thrush

Hylocichla mustelina

Wood Thrushes, the best-known eastern spotted thrushes, frequent moist woodlots throughout the Southeast in summer. These noted songsters often visit wooded lawns and gardens.

You can attract Wood Thrushes to your backyard by including berry-producing shrubs in your naturescape and providing water.

Ron Austing

Identification Flashes and Distinguishing Features:

Their rufous-red upperparts and black-spotted underparts distinguish Wood Thrushes from other birds.

Size: 7¾–8½ inches (20–21.5 centimeters)

Color: Both males and females have rich rufous-red crowns, napes, and backs, olive brown rumps and tails, and white underparts that are heavily spotted with large, round black markings. They have pink legs.

Voice: They make musical flute-like to bell-like songs of phrases of rapid *pit-pit-pit* notes that rise in pitch and then fall. In early morning and at dusk they make *ee-oh-lee, ee-oh-lay* calls.

Range: They are summer residents throughout the Southeast except the Louisiana delta and areas south of the coastal plain in the Florida peninsula.

Habitat: They prefer cool, humid deciduous forests, parks, gardens, and wooded urban areas. Females build robinlike nesting cups on crotches of branches using leaves, mosses, grasses, mud, and sometimes paper. They line their nests with rootlets (robins use grasses).

Eggs: They lay 2–5 pale-blue to blue-green eggs; 2 broods per breeding season. The female incubates the eggs, and the male guards the nest whenever the female leaves; incubation takes 13–14 days. Fledglings leave the nest 13–14 days after hatching.

Food: They eat primarily insects and other small invertebrates that they forage on the ground or glean from foliage (earthworms, ants, beetles, crickets, spiders, moths, and caterpillars). They also eat fruit and berries, especially in fall.

Habits: Like other thrushes, they sing beautiful songs; you will hear their best songs at dusk. They have become more accepting of people and often build nests close to homes in residential, wooded neighborhoods. When alarmed, they raise their head feathers into a crest.

American Robin
Turdus migratorius

Fred J. Alsop III

American Robins are the largest North American thrushes and among the the the best-known birds on the North American continent. Even young children recognize "Robin Redbreast." These large songbirds frequent our lawns and have even become urban dwellers.

You can attract American Robins to your backyard by including lawn areas and berry-producing plants in your naturescape, nesting shelves or ledges (see Habitat, below) and providing water. They especially enjoy birdbaths, pools, and running water.

Identification Flashes and Distinguishing Features:

Their large size and distinctive orange-red breasts make American Robins easy to identify.

Size: 9–11 inches (23–28 centimeters)

Color: Males have gray-brown upperparts with black heads, tails, and wings and white rings around their eyes. They have chestnut to brick-red breasts and bellies, white lower bellies and undertail coverts, white tail corners, and yellow bills; their throats are streaked white and black. Females are paler versions of the males, and juveniles are similar to their parents but with underparts heavily spotted with black.

Voice: They sing a back-and-forth *cheer-up, cheer, cheer, cheerily cheer-up*. They also make loud *hip, hip, hip* or *hup, hup, hup* calls.

Range: They are permanent residents across the Southeast.

Habitat: They frequent open woods, farmlands, and parks and gardens in urban areas. Females build bulky nesting cups in the forks or on horizontal branches of deciduous trees or conifers and sometimes on ledges or "nesting shelves" placed on the side of a building. They work grasses, string, cloth, paper, and weeds into the mud interlinings of their nests and then line the finished nests with fine grasses.

Eggs: They lay 3–6 unmarked "robin's-egg blue" eggs; 2–3 broods per breeding season. The female incubates the eggs; incubation takes 12–14 days. Fledglings leave the nest 14–16 days after hatching.

Food: They eat primarily earthworms found by sight on lawns, golf courses, and fields; they also eat grasshoppers, crickets, moths, cicadas, beetles, caterpillars, butterflies, weevils, cutworms, termites, and ants. They occasionally eat fruit and berries (dogwood, bayberries, pokeberries, and chinaberries) and will come to feeders for mealworms or bread.

Habits: The males are very territorial and often fight each other or their own reflections in windows, mirrors, or the chrome on cars.

Gray Catbird
Dumetella carolinensis

These tame little birds live in shrubbery, and their genus namd, *Dumetella*, refers to a "thicket dweller." Although they are members of the Mockingbird family, they aren't as good at mimicry as their cousins.

You can attract Gray Catbirds to your backyard by including shrubbery in your naturescape, providing water, and offering raisins, cheese, nuts, and cereals.

Fred J. Alsop III

Identification Flashes and Distinguishing Features:

Look for the black crowns and tails on their gray bodies.

Size: 8½ inches (22 centimeters)

Color: They have dark slate-gray bodies, black caps, long black tails, and reddish undertail coverts.

Voice: They make mockingbird-like phrases, but with no repetition of phrases. They mix catlike *meow* or down-slurred *mew* sounds into their songs. Sometimes they mimic frogs and other birds.

Range: They are summer residents north of the coastal plains; permanent residents on the East Gulf, South Atlantic, and Mid-Atlantic Coastal Plains; and winter visitors on the East Gulf Coastal Plain, across Florida, and sometimes farther north.

Habitat: They prefer woodland undergrowth, hedgerows, thickets, gardens, and ornamental plantings. The female, with the help of her mate, builds a deep nesting cup with a bulky foundation of vines, twigs, weeds, grasses, and bark strips and lined with rootlets, hair, fine grasses, and pine needles.

Eggs: They lay 2–6 deep bluish-green unmarked eggs; 2 broods per breeding season. The female incubates the eggs; incubation takes 13–15 days. Fledglings leave the nest 10–15 days after hatching.

Food: About half of their diet consists of insects (caterpillars, moths, crickets, June beetles, Japanese beetles, cicadas, dragonflies, centipedes, and spiders). They also eat fruit and berries (dogwood, grapes, blackberries, and blueberries). They will come to feeders for cheese, raisins, peanuts, boiled potatoes, and cereals.

Habits: These often fearless birds allow close approach, sometimes becoming tame to the continued presence of people in their territory. If you make "squeaking" or "pishing" sounds with your hands, they will quickly come to investigate.

Brown Thrasher

Toxostoma rufum

Ron Austing

Although Brown Thrashers are not the mimics that Gray Catbirds or Northern Mockingbirds are, they are excellent songsters and occasionally mimic parts of the songs of other birds. They frequently sing from high, exposed perches. These large reddish-brown birds often forage on the ground, sometimes dashing across the road like miniature roadrunners.

You can attract Brown Thrashers to your backyard by including thick shrubbery in your naturescape and providing water.

Identification Flashes and Distinguishing Features:

Their large size, rufous-red upperparts, streaked underparts, and long tails distinguish Brown Thrashers from other birds.

Size: 10½–12 inches (27–30.5 centimeters)

Color: Both males and females have rich rufous-red upperparts, white to buff underparts that are heavily streaked with dark brown to black, long, dark decurved bills, yellow eyes (adults), long rounded tails, and white wing bars.

Voice: They make mockingbird-like phrases, repeating each phrase 2–3 times. They also make loud *smack* notes.

Range: They are summer residents across the Southeast and permanent residents on the coastal plains from the Upper East Gulf Coastal Plain south along the Gulf Coast and all of Florida, as well as north along the Mid-Atlantic Coastal Plain.

Habitat: They frequent the edges of woodlots, old brushy fields, overgrown fencerows and hedgerows, farmlands, roadsides, brier patches, and gardens. Both parents build nesting cups close to the ground in dense thickets, low tangles, shrubs, and low trees. Their nests often have 4 levels: a base of larger twigs topped with layers of leaves, smaller twigs, and coarse grasses.

Eggs: They lay 3–6 pale-blue to white eggs that are covered with small reddish-brown spots; 2 broods per breeding season. Both parents incubate the eggs; incubation takes 12–14 days. Fledglings leave the nest 9–13 days after hatching.

Food: They usually forage on the ground, using their bills to dig in the soil and turn over leaves to expose food. About 70 percent of their diet consists of insects and other invertebrates. They also take small salamanders, frogs, snakes, and lizards. They occasionally feed on fruit, berries, acorns, and waste corn.

Habits: They are often loud and musical. They aggressively defend their young, sometimes flying at the head of an intruder. They tolerate people and frequent yards and gardens.

Northern Mockingbird

Mimus polyglottos

They are noted for their mimicry of other birds' calls as well as for their ability to incorporate these and other sounds (roosters' crows, dogs' barking, piano notes, machines, frogs, police whistles, etc.) into their songs. They sing day and night during the breeding season.

Ron Austing

You can attract Northern Mockingbirds to your backyard by including berry-producing plants in your naturescape, providing water, and filling feeders with suet, suet mixes, fruit, or bread.

Identification Flashes and Distinguishing Features:

Look for the white flash spots and the white edge on the long tails of these basically grayish birds.

Size: 9–11 inches (23-28 centimeters)

Color: Both males and females have medium-gray upperparts, pale-gray to whitish underparts, darker gray to blackish wings and tails, large white patches on their wings, and white outer tail feathers. Juveniles have heavily spotted underparts.

Voice: They make loud, abrupt *check* calls as well as rich, varied songs composed of phrases, including mimicry of other birds and sounds, repeated 3–5 times in a row. Displaying birds often "leap" into the air from a high perch and sing both on the way up and on the way back down. Females sing in fall to establish their winter territory.

Range: They are permanent residents throughout the Southeast.

Habitat: They frequent trees, shrubs, and vines. Both parents build their nesting cup low to the ground using twigs for the outer layer and leaves, vines, wool, string, paper, fine grasses, rootlets, and hair for the lining.

Eggs: They lay 3–6 blue-and-green eggs that are heavily marked with brown spots and blotches; 2–3 broods per breeding season. The female incubates the eggs; incubation takes 12–13 days. Fledglings leave the nest 10–12 days after hatching.

Food: Almost 60 percent of their diet consists of animal foods (insects, worms, spiders, snails, frogs, lizards, and small snakes). They also eat fruit and berries and will come to feeders for suet, raisins, cut apples, or bread.

Habits: In the spring males sing most of the day and sometimes well into the night. They aggressively defend their young and often dive at intruders, including people, cats, and dogs. They also defend their winter territory to protect food supplies. When foraging on the ground, they often spread their wings with a jerk above their backs to startle insects into moving, making them easy prey.

Cedar Waxwing
Bombycilla cedrorum

Ron Austing

Flocks of these sleek brown-crested birds with their black masks appear to fill fall dogwoods, early spring holly trees, or spring blossoming apple trees. In a few hours or days, they may be gone just as quickly as they arrived, following their erratic path to the next bounty of fruit. They are named for the drop-shaped red tip that forms on the secondary wing feathers—and sometimes tails—of adults—this tip resembles the red wax that was once used to seal letters.

You can attract Cedar Waxwings by including plants that bear small fruit or berries in your naturescape. You can also attract them by providing water.

Identification Flashes and Distinguishing Features:

Look for the distinctive yellow-tipped tails on these crested grayish birds.

Size: 7–8 inches (18-20 centimeters)

Color: The colors on these elegant birds blend into one another like wet watercolor. Both males and females have brown crests; pale-brownish upper breasts, heads, and backs; pale yellow lower breasts and bellies; and blue-grayish wings, rumps, and upper tails. They have white undertail coverts, and the outer halves of their tails are dark with a bright yellow terminal band. Most adults have red tips on their secondary wing feathers. They have black masks that extend from their foreheads through their lores to behind their eyes.

Voice: They emit high-pitched trilled *hziss, hzisss, hzisss* whistles.

Range: They are permanent residents on the Interior Low Plateau, the Cumberlands and Southern Ridge and Valley, the Southern Blue Ridge, and the western edges of the Piedmont. They winter throughout the Southeast.

Habitat: They nest in open stands of scattered trees or in shrubs and place their nesting cups in forks or on horizontal limbs. Both parents carry grasses, twigs, weeds, mosses, string, lichens, and plant fibers to the nesting site, where the female weaves them into a cup and lines it with rootlets, fine grasses, and hair.

Eggs: They lay 2–6 pale-gray to bluish-gray eggs lightly coated with small black dots; 1–2 broods per breeding season. The female incubates the eggs; incubation takes 12–18 days. Fledglings leave the nest 14–16 days after hatching.

Food: In the summer they eat primarily insects taken on the wing flycatcher-fashion. They also eat fruit, berries, sap, and petals. In late summer they may get drunk on fermented fruit.

Habits: Nomadic wandering flocks search for new food sources, and they occasionally nest in loosely formed colonies. During courting they pass flower petals back and forth, and when feeding several birds may perch side by side and pass a berry or cherry back and forth until one of them eats it.

European Starling
Sturnus vulgaris

Ron Austing

These Eurasian songbirds were introduced into New York City in the late-
nineteenth century, and in the past hundred
years they've become established in many
parts of North America. These aggressive
generalists seem perfectly adapted to settle
a new world and have been most effective in
doing so. They greatly benefit farmers by eating destructive insects in large numbers.

You can attract European Starlings by providing water and filling feeders with
suet, suet mixes, or table scraps. They will aggressively seek and defend nesting
sites and will accept nesting boxes with holes at least 1½ inches in diameter.

Identification Flashes and Distinguishing Features:

Their short tails and squatty appearance make it easy to
distinguish European Starlings from other black birds. Also,
they walk instead of hopping.

Size: 8½ inches (22 centimeters)

Color: During breeding season both males and females have shiny
oily greenish-purple plumage and yellow bills. The rest of
the year they have dark bills and blacker plumage with white
spots and crescent-shaped markings. Juveniles have dark bills
and ashy gray-brown plumage with white throats.

Voice: They sing cascades of squeaky chatter, twitters, chirps, and
pheeweWWe ("wolf whistle") sounds. They imitate the calls
and songs of pewees, bobwhites, killdeers, and phoebes.

Range: They are permanent residents throughout the Southeast.

Habitat: These secondary-cavity nesters look for natural cavities,
woodpecker holes (which they aggressively commandeer),
holes in buildings, pipes, and nesting boxes with entrance
holes at least 1½ inches in diameter. They build loosely
constructed nesting cups from grass, straw, paper, leaves,
weeds, debris, and cloth. They line their nests with finer
grasses, hair, and feathers.

Eggs: They lay 2–8 pale-blue or greenish-white eggs that are usually
unmarked; 2–3 broods per breeding season. Both parents
incubate the eggs; incubation takes 12–14 days. Fledglings
leave the nest about 21 days after hatching.

Food: They forage on the ground for a variety of insects and other
invertebrates (clover weevil, cutworms, Japanese beetles,
grasshoppers, snails, spiders, and earthworms). They also
eat fruit and berries as well as weed seeds and grain. They
occasionally forage in garbage and will come to feeders for
small grains, suet, suet mixes, and bread.

Habits: They often flutter their wings rapidly during singing displays.
They aggressively compete for nesting sites. Mixed-species
flocks of starlings, blackbirds, and robins may number into
the hundreds of thousands or even millions.

Red-eyed Vireo
Vireo olivaceus

Ron Austing

Once considered the most abundant eastern woodland bird in the summer, the Red-eyed Vireo, like so many migratory songbirds, is declining in numbers. These birds are not noted for the beauty of their song but rather for the persistence of the singers, who serenade from dawn through the hottest part of summer days and into dusk. These long sermons have earned them the name "preacher birds." One Red-eyed Vireo was recorded to sing more than 22,000 renditions in a single summer day!

You can attract Red-eyed Vireos to your backyard by including large deciduous trees in your naturescape and providing water.

Identification Flashes and Distinguishing Features:

The dark line "through" their eyes, the white line above their eyes, and the lack of wing bars help distinguish Red-eyed Vireos from other birds. If you can get within close range, look for their distinctive red eyes.

Size: 6 inches (15 centimeters)

Color: They have olive-green upperparts and white underparts with yellow tints on their undertail coverts; there are no bars on their wings. They have white stripes over their eyes and black stripes "through" their eyes and along their gray crowns. Adult birds have red eyes that can be seen at close range.

Voice: They make nasal *jmew* notes and sing long series of phrases and pauses, mostly in middle tones, in the pattern of *look up, see me? over here, this way, higher still,* etc.

Range: They are summer residents over the entire Southeast except peninsular and Tropical Florida.

Habitat: They frequent open deciduous woodlands that have thick sapling undergrowth, wooded clearings, wooded residential areas, and gardens. Females build well-constructed hanging nesting cups in the forks of slender horizontal tree branches. They bind together grasses, vine tendrils, bark strips, rootlets, and paper from wasp's nests with spider and tent caterpillar silks. They decorate the finished nesting cups with lichens.

Eggs: They lay 2–5 white eggs sparsely marked on the large end with black and brown dots and spots; 1 brood per breeding season. The female incubates the eggs; incubation takes 11–14 days. Fledglings leave the nest 10–12 days after hatching.

Food: They feed mostly on insects gleaned from trees (bees, wasps, ants, caterpillars, moths, webworms, beetles, spiders, and scale insects). They also take some fruit and berries (elderberry, spicebush, magnolia, dogwood, and sassafras).

Habits: Except for nesting, Red-eyed Vireos stay in the treetops, but once you learn their song, you will be able to spot them. During summer they will be almost anywhere there are trees.

Yellow-rumped (Myrtle) Warbler

Dendroica coronata

These conspicuous birds often draw attention to themselves with their loud calls and their habit of darting out of branches to hawk passing insects. Their bright-yellow rump patches (they are often called "butter butts") will help you identify them. Their wing tips often conceal their rump patches when the birds are perched, but the yellow flashes will be highly visible as they flit from branch and fly.

Ron Austing

You can attract them by including berry-producing plants in your naturescape, providing water, and offering suet or doughnuts.

Identification Flashes and Distinguishing Features:

Their small size, streaked underparts, and bright-yellow rump patches help distinguish Yellow-rumped Warblers.

Size: 5½ inches (14 centimeters)

Color: Breeding males have gray-black upperparts, grey-black faces, black chests, white streaks on their sides and flanks, white chins, throats, wing bars, broken eye rings, narrow eye stripes, and yellow patches on the sides of their chests, crowns, and rumps. Breeding females look like washed-out males. In winter both males and females have brown upperparts with yellow rump patches and streaked-brown underparts.

Voice: They most often make loud *check!* sounds. Their spring migration song is a musical trill that is weaker in the middle and often sung in 2 parts, with the second part at a higher pitch.

Range: They are common winter visitors and rare summer residents throughout the Southeast, but they breed only as far south as the Southern Blue Ridge forests.

Habitat: They can be found in a variety of temperate vegetation and habitats. They nest in conifer trees at high elevations and build their nesting cups on horizontal branches, often near the trunk, using twigs, bark strips, plant down, and fibers. They line their nests with finer grasses and hair and cover the eggs with lots of feathers when the female leaves the nest.

Eggs: They lay 3–5 white or creamy-white eggs spotted and blotched with browns at the large end, often in a wreath design; 1 brood per breeding season. The female incubates the eggs; incubation takes 11–13 days. Fledglings leave the nest 12–14 days after hatching.

Food: In summer they eat small insects and spiders gleaned from trees, by flycatching, and by foraging on the ground. In winter they eat primarily berries and small seeds. They will come to feeders for suet, peanut butter-suet mixes, and doughnuts.

Habits: They are the most common wintering warblers over most of the Southeast and are often seen in conspicuous flocks.

Ron Austing

Pine Warbler

Dendroica pinus

Fittingly named, Pine Warblers are almost always found in open pine stands. Only populations north of the Piedmont and Upper East Gulf Coastal Plain are migratory, joining others in the Southeast in late fall.

You can attract Pine Warblers to your backyard by including pine trees in your naturescape, providing water, and filling feeders with suet, peanut butter-suet mixes, or cornmeal mixes.

Ron Austing

Ron Austing

Identification Flashes and Distinguishing Features:

Look for their greenish upperparts, yellow breasts, and white bellies.

Size: 5½ inches (14 centimeters)

Color: Males are olive-green from head to rump, with darker olive-green wings and tails. They have greenish-yellow to yellow chins, throats, breasts, and upper bellies with some dark streaking; white lower bellies and undertail coverts; yellow stripes over their eyes; and white wing bars. Females look the same but paler.

Voice: Males sing soft, low-pitched lazy trills year-round that sounds like the Chipping Sparrow's song but with softer, lower, slower notes that change in pitch, loudness, and cadence.

Range: They are permanent residents in the Southeast except the Southern Blue Ridge area, northern and central Tennessee, and extreme South Florida; they are summer residents everywhere except southernmost tip of Florida.

Habitat: They frequent open pine woods and saddle their compact nesting cups on horizontal branches or in clusters of needles. They make their nests from weeds, barks, pine twigs, and pine needles bound together with spider and caterpillar silks and lined with plant down, pine needles, feathers, and hair.

Eggs: They lay 3–5 white, grayish, or greenish-white eggs with brown spots and splotches in a wreath around the large ends; 2–3 broods per breeding season. The female incubates the eggs; incubation takes 12–13 days. It's unknown when the fledglings leave the nest.

Food: They eat primarily insects (beetles, cotton-boll weevil, moths, caterpillars, grasshoppers, scale insects, and spiders). They also eat seeds and berries. They will come to feeders for suet, peanut butter-suet mixes, and cornmeal mixtures.

Habits: They nest as early as March. They hawk flying insects like a flycatcher, launching from the tips of branches. Sometimes they feed on the ground.

Ron Austing

Palm Warbler

Dendroica palmarum

Other than frequenting saw palmettos in Florida in winter, the misnamed Palm Warblers are seldom found in palms. They nest in the bogs in boreal forests in the northern United States and southern Canada.

You can attract Palm Warblers to your backyard by including low berry-producing shrubs in your naturescape and providing water.

Ron Austing

Ron Austing

Identification Flashes and Distinguishing Features:

Look for their constant up-and-down tail-wagging behavior and their yellow rumps and undertail coverts.

Size: 5½ inches (14 centimeters)

Color: In breeding season males have chestnut caps, brownish upperparts with dark streaking, yellowish underparts with chestnut streaking, yellow undertail coverts, yellowish rumps, white lines over eyes, dark lines "through" eyes, and whitish wing bars. They lose their chestnut coloring after breeding season, and their underparts become white to gray with yellow undertail coverts. Females look like post-breeding males but paler.

Voice: They sing buzzy Junco-like or Chipping Sparrow-like trills.

Range: They winter on the Gulf and Atlantic Coastal Plains and in Florida; they breed in northern United States and southern Canada and migrate through the Southeast in spring and fall.

Habitat: They frequent brushy fencerows, shrub-scrub areas, gardens, brushy undergrowth, and marshy areas with cattail stands; they nest in bogs and hummocks of lichens and mosses on the ground. Females build nests under small trees and shrubs. They make their nests with bark, weed stalks, and grasses and line them with finer grasses, feathers, and rootlets.

Eggs: They lay 3–5 white to creamy-white eggs dotted, spotted and blotched with brown often in wreath pattern around larger end; 2 broods per breeding season. The female incubates the eggs; incubation takes about 12 days. Fledglings leave the nest 12–13 days after hatching.

Food: They eat primarily insects (cotton worms, gnats, ants, caterpillars, beetles, mosquitoes, aphids, crickets, spiders, and grasshoppers). They also eat small berries (bayberries, raspberries, and poison ivy).

Habits: They usually forage on or near the ground, sometimes higher in trees. They are easily noticed near low shrubbery. They wag their tails slowly up and down.

Yellow-throated Warbler

Dendroica dominica

Since this bright-yellow throated warbler perfers to forage in treetops, it often escapes attention until its foraging brings it to ground level. If you learn its distinctive song, you will know that Yellow-throated Warblers are nearby even though you may not see them.

You can attract Yellow-throated Warblers to your backyard by including tall trees in your naturescape, providing water, and filling feeders with suet, suet mixes, or bread crumbs.

Ron Austing

Identification Flashes and Distinguishing Features:

Listen for their distinctive song. Look for their bright-yellow throats, black faces, and bold white lines over their eyes.

Size: 5½ inches (14 centimeters)

Color: Both males and females have gray upperparts, white underparts, bright-yellow throats, black faces (female has less black), wide white stripes over eyes, white ear patches, white wing bars, and black streaks on flanks.

Voice: They make series of double *teetle, teetle, tadle, tadle, tadle, tee* notes trailing off down the scale and rising at the end.

Range: They are summer residents north of Florida and southeastern tip of Georgia; permanent residents in southeastern Georgia and northern Florida; winter visitors in Tropical Florida.

Habitat: They frequent live oaks, cypress trees, sycamores, and pines along waterways, on bottomlands and swamps, and in ridgetop forests. They are attracted to Spanish moss. Females build nests in Spanish moss in coastal areas; inland birds saddle nests on horizontal branches. They make nests from bark strips, mosses, grasses, and weed stems and line them with grasses, moss, plant fibers and down, and feathers.

Eggs: They lay 3–5 greenish-white to grayish-white eggs speckled and blotched with grays, browns, lavenders, and wine reds often in wreath pattern at large end; 2 broods per breeding season. The female incubates the eggs; incubation takes 12–13 days. It's unknown when fledgings leave the nest.

Food: They eat primarily insects (moths, caterpillars, ants, flies, scale insects, aphids, mosquitoes, grasshoppers, crickets, houseflies, spiders, and beetles). They will come to feeders for suet, peanut butter-suet mixes, and bread crumbs.

Habits: They live in treetops, and creep along main branches and the trunk foraging for insects. They also hawk insects midair from treetop perches. Among the earliest birds to migrate northward, they reach northeast Tennessee and western North Carolina in late March or early April.

Northern Cardinal

Cardinalis cardinalis

Ron Austing

Named for the red-robed Roman Catholic dignitaries, Northern Cardinals have been selected as the official bird of seven states. Among the most recognized and popular birds of the eastern United States, they live in a great variety of habitats.

You can attract Northern Cardinals to your backyard by including shrubbery in your naturescape and providing water. They will become regular visitors at feeders filled with sunflower seeds.

Identification Flashes and Distinguishing Features:

Male cardinals are the only bright-red birds with crests. Female cardinals are the only red-billed birds with crests.

Size: 7½–8½ inches (19–22 centimeters)

Color: Males have brilliant red plumage, thick reddish beaks, crests, and black faces. Females have olive-gray upperparts, bronzy golden-buff underparts, and reddish bills, wings, crests, and tails. Juveniles look like "browner" females with dark bills.

Voice: They make sharp *chip* notes and widely varied songs of rich, whistled notes in three common patterns: *whoit, cheer, cheer; cheer; cheer, whoit, whoit, whoit, whoit;* and *cheer, pret-ty, pret-ty, pret-ty.* They sing year-round; the males' song is stronger.

Range: They are permanent residents across the Southeast.

Habitat: They live in a variety of habitats: shrubbery, open woodlands, thickets, brushy areas, forest edges, groves, parks, forests, and suburban gardens. Females build deep nesting cups in thick shrubs or low in small trees. They make their nests from twigs, vines, leaves, weeds, coarse grasses, bark, paper, and string and line them with finer grasses, rootlets, and hair.

Eggs: They lay 2–5 grayish, greenish, or bluish-white eggs heavily blotched and spotted with grays, browns, and purples; 2–4 broods per breeding season; male often takes care of 1 brood while female incubates subsequent clutches of eggs; incubation takes 12–13 days. Fledglings leave the nest 10–11 days after hatching.

Food: They feed on more than 50 kinds of medium to large insects and more than 30 kinds of seeds, fruit, and berries. They also eat waste corn, tree buds, blossoms, and grains. They will come to feeders for sunflower seeds and cracked corn.

Habits: They forage on or near the ground. Males are strongly territorial; when winter flocks break up, they repeatedly attack their reflections, which they mistake for rival males, in windows, mirrors, car bumpers, and hubcaps. They are attracted to birdbaths. They can lower their red crests at will.

Ron Austing

Rose-breasted Grosbeak
Pheucticus ludovicianus

These showy cardinal-size finches are becoming more common visitors in the Southeast during their northward migration each spring. They frequent gardens in northern areas of their range and have earned the nickname "potato-bug birds."

You can attract Rose-breasted Grosbeaks to your backyard by providing water and filling feeders with sunflower seeds.

Ron Austing

Ron Austing

Identification Flashes and Distinguishing Features:

Look for the rosy red breast on the black-and-white males and large conical bills and the wing bars on the buffy-tan females.

Size: 7–8½ inches (18–22 centimeters)

Color: Males have black heads and upperparts; white rumps, corner tail feathers, wing patches, and underparts; rosy red breasts (brownish on 1–2 year-olds) and inner wing linings; large, thick, and white to straw-colored bills. Females and juveniles have dark brownish-black upperparts, white throats, white lines "through" eyes extending back to necks, buffy-white underparts heavily streaked with black, and yellow wing linings.

Voice: They make sharp *peek* notes and beautiful, clear, sweet robinlike singsong patterns. Males often sing from the nest; females sing softer.

Range: They are common spring and fall migrating visitors across the Southeast and breeding and summer residents in the Southern Blue Ridge area.

Habitat: They frequent thickets, moist deciduous woodlands, swamps, orchards, and suburban areas in summer. During migration they can be found anywhere there are broad-leafed trees. Both parents build a poorly constructed nesting cup in shrubs or forks of small trees. They make their nests from weed stems, small twigs and straw and line them with finer grasses, rootlets, and hair.

Eggs: They lay 3–6 bluish, grayish, or greenish eggs with spots and blotches of browns, grays, and purples often concentrated at the large end. Both parents incubate the eggs; incubation takes 12–14 days. Fledgings leave the nest 9–12 days after hatching.

Food: They eat the seeds and blossoms of elm, hickory, and beech trees as well as insects (potato beetles, locusts, cankerworms, grasshoppers, and moths). They will come to feeders for sunflower seeds.

Habits: Males sing from their nest and often appear affectionate; courting pairs often touch bills. They frequent feeders in May during spring migration.

Ron Austing

Indigo Bunting
Passerina cyanea

These sparrow-size birds frequently perch on utility wires, fly up from highways into roadside thickets, and visit feeders during winter months and migrations. In strong light males appear to be a brilliant, iridescent indigo blue; in poor light or when backlighted, they may look black.

You can attract Indigo Buntings to your backyard by including hedges and thickets in your naturescape, providing water, and filling feeders with sunflower seeds.

Ron Austing

Identification Flashes and Distinguishing Features:

Male Indigo Buntings are the only dark-blue sparrow-size birds seen in the Southeast. Their brilliant indigo-blue plumage makes them easy to identify.

Size: 5½ inches (14 centimeters)

Color: Males at least 2 years old have bright indigo-blue bodies with blue to purplish heads and rusty wingbars; bellies of younger males have patches of brown and sometimes white. Females and juveniles are rich brown without obvious streaking; female heads may have slight crested appearance.

Voice: They sing varied high-pitched phrases, with the beginning phrases paired and often followed by a short trilled *sweet-sweet, sweeter-sweeter, here-here*. They also make wet *tsick* sounds, as if they're trying to spit out feathers.

Range: They are summer residents and breeding birds over the Southeast except the southernmost tip of Florida. Some of them winter in the Southeast; most winter in southern Florida.

Habitat: They frequent overgrown fencerows, brushy weedy areas, agricultural areas, woodland edges, disturbed edges, roadside thickets, hedges, and clearings for utility wires. Females build nests close to the ground in the crotches of saplings, thickets, brier patches, weed stems, and canebreaks. They make well-woven nesting cups of grasses, weed stems, bark fibers, Spanish moss, and paper on a base of leaves or sometimes snake skin. They line their nests with finer grasses, hair, feathers, plant down, and rootlets.

Eggs: They lay 2–6 unmarked white eggs; 2 broods per breeding season. The female incubates the eggs; incubation takes 12–13 days. Fledglings leave the nest 8–10 days after hatching.

Food: They eat insects (grasshoppers, caterpillars, cicadas, beetles, weevils, flies, cankerworms, mosquitoes, and spiders), plant foods (seeds of grasses, goldenrod, dandelion, thistle, and small grains), and small fruit and berries (elderberries, black-berries, and privet berries). They will come to feeders for black oil sunflower seeds, millet, and safflower seeds.

Habits: They are persistent singers and often sing from shaded perches through the heat of summer days. Males often sing while displaying in a slow flight with rapidly beating wings.

Ron Austing

Ron Austing

Painted Bunting
Passerina ciris

Once sold on streets as a cage bird, Painted Buntings were called "nonpareil"—the incomparable. The males are among the most colorful of Southern songbirds.

You can attract Painted Buntings to your backyard by providing water and filling feeders with millet and other small grains.

Ron Austing

Identification Flashes and Distinguishing Features:

The males are unmistakable—no other buntings or other birds have such colorful plumage. The females are the only small green finches seen in the Southeast.

Size: 5½ inches (14 centimeters)

Color: Males at least 2 years old have blue heads, yellow-green backs, purplish-red rumps, red underparts and eye rings, and green-washed wings and tails; 1-year-old males are mostly green with blue head patches. Females have green upperparts and yellow-green underparts. Juveniles are drab brown with greenish washes.

Voice: They sing sweet, high-pitched, thin-spaced *you-eta, you-eta, I eaty you too* notes.

Range: They are summer residents and breeding birds on the South Carolina South Atlantic and Mid-Atlantic Coastal Plains, Mississippi Gulf Coastal Plain, and Mississippi River Alluvial Plain northward into Tennessee. They are winter visitors in Tropical Florida.

Habitat: They frequent open country, brushy weed-grown fields, gardens, railroad clearings, roadside thickets, woodland edges, and riparian thickets. They build their nests close to the ground in trees, thick brush, or vines. They make well-woven cups of leaves topped with dried grasses, bark, and weed stalks and lined with finer grasses, rootlets, and hair.

Eggs: They lay 3–5 pale bluish-white eggs with brown spots; 2–4 broods per breeding season. The female incubates the eggs; incubation takes 11–12 days. Fledglings leave the nest 12–14 days after hatching.

Food: They eat primarily small seeds of grasses but also take some insects (boll weevils, grasshoppers, wasps, caterpillars, crickets, and spiders). They will come to feeders for millet and other small grains and "wild bird" mixes.

Habits: They sing from exposed perches atop low shrubs, small trees, or utility wires. They are often shy and retiring. Males are polygamous and often fiercely combat rival males to the point of injury—most unusual behavior for birds.

Eastern (Rufous-sided) Towhee

Pipilo erythrophthalmus

They are often called Ground Robins because of their robinlike appearance, or Cheewinks because of their call notes. They frequent thickets and forage on the ground, making lots of noise as they rake over dried leaves with a "double-scratch" (kicking backward with both feet at the same time).

You can attract Eastern Towhees to your backyard by providing water and offering small seeds either on the ground or on platform feeders low to the ground.

Fred J. Alsop III

Identification Flashes and Distinguishing Features:

Look for the black upperparts and rufous sides of male Eastern Towhees and the brown upperparts and rufous sides of the females.

Size: 7–8¾ inches (18-22 centimeters)

Color: Males have black upperparts with large white corner tail patches; rufous sides, flanks, and undertail coverts; and white bellies. Females have brown instead of black plumage. Except for Florida races, both males and females have red eyes.

Voice: They make sharp, loud *cheewink* or *towhee* sounds. Male song resembles *drink-your-tea-ee-ee-ee-ee* with much variation and often omitting first or last notes.

Range: They are permanent residents across the Southeast.

Habitat: They frequent barrens, open brushy fields, thickets, roadside edges, farmlands, parks, residential areas with ornamental plantings, gardens, hedgerows, and young clearcuts. Females build bulky nesting cups on or near the ground. They make their nests from bark, grasses, weeds, twigs, leaves, and string and line them with finer grasses, hair, pine needles, and rootlets.

Eggs: They lay 2–6 creamy-white to pale-gray eggs with reddish-brown dots or spots; 2–3 broods per breeding season. The female incubates the eggs; incubation takes 12–13 days. Fledglings leave the nest 10–12 days after hatching.

Food: They forage on the ground and eat spiders, millipedes, snails, earthworms, lizards, salamanders, and small snakes. They also eat fruit, berries, and seeds of weeds and grasses. They will come to feeders for black oil sunflower seeds or millet.

Habits: Cowbirds frequently parasitize towhees by laying eggs in their nests so the towhees will raise the cowbird young. During breeding season males often sing from high, exposed perches. They live alone, either singly or in pairs.

Chipping Sparrow
Spizella passerina

Ron Austing

Chipping Sparrows rank among the smallest and most common backyard sparrows. They require short, sparse grass for foraging.

You can attract Chipping Sparrows to your backyard by including lawn areas as well as dense shrubbery in your naturescape, providing water, and filling feeders with millet and other small seeds.

Identification Flashes and Distinguishing Features:

Look for their chestnut crowns, unmarked underparts, white stripes over their eyes, and black lines "through" their eyes.

Size: 5½ inches (14 centimeters)

Color: Adults have streaked brown upperparts, white throats, white stripes over their eyes, black lines "through" their eyes, gray faces, grayish unstreaked underparts, dark bills, and whitish wing bars. During breeding season, adults have chestnut caps. Juveniles have streaked crowns and underparts.

Voice: They make one of the easiest songs to learn: a series of *chip-chip-chip-chip-chip-chip-chip* notes all on the same pitch, like a small machine gun.

Range: They are summer residents north of the Piedmont, permanent residents from south of the Piedmont across the Southeast except the southernmost Gulf Coastal Plain and Florida. They are winter visitors in Florida.

Habitat: They frequent open grassy woodlands, pine woodlands, parks, orchards, grassy fields, gardens, towns, farmlands, suburbs, and Christmas tree farms. Males help the females build nests in conifer and other trees, shrubs, and vines. They make well-woven nesting cups from dead grasses, rootlets, and weed stems and line them with finer grasses and hairs from horses, dogs, cattle, and people.

Eggs: They lay 2–5 pale-blue eggs with dark brown, black, gray, and blue splotches in wreath around the larger end; 2 broods per breeding season. The female incubates the eggs, and the male feeds her while she is on the nest; incubation takes 11–14 days. Fledglings leave nest 8–11 days after hatching.

Food: They feed on small insects and small seeds. They will come to feeders for millet and other small grains.

Habits: They are tame and approachable and will learn to accept food from your hand. Cowbirds frequently parasitize towhees by laying eggs in their nests so the towhees will raise the cowbird young.

Field Sparrow
Spizella pusilla

These small, slender, long-tailed birds are often seen in old fields and thickets. Their song can be heard in rural areas during the day and on moonlit summer nights. Their populations seem to be decreasing over much of their range, perhaps due to changes in their habitat, particularly the turning under of weedy fields in the winter and the clearing of brushy fencerows.

You can attract Field Sparrows to your backyard by providing water and filling feeders with millet and other small seeds.

Ron Austing

Ron Austing

Ron Austing

Identification Flashes and Distinguishing Features:

Look for their unmarked underparts, white eye rings, and pink bills.

Size: 5¾ inches (15 centimeters)

Color: They have brownish, dark-streaked upperparts; unstreaked grayish-buff underparts; gray faces with brown stripes behind their eyes; white eye rings and wing bars; and pink bills.

Voice: They sing a series of clear, plaintive whistles that starts slow and evenly spaced but accelerates until it fades, like a ball bouncing faster and faster until it stops.

Range: They are permanent residents across the Southeast except the Florida peninsula, where they winter (they do not go farther south).

Habitat: They frequent old fields and thickets, abandoned farmlands, brier patches, young pine plantations, old clearcuts, clearings, and brushy pastures. They sometimes nest on or near the ground; other times they build elevated nests in blackberry tangles, small conifers, bushes, weed patches, and saplings. Males help the females make open nesting cups from dead grasses, weed stems, and leaves; they line their nests with finer grasses, rootlets, and hair, especially horsehair.

Eggs: They lay 2–6 creamy-white, bluish-white, or greenish-white eggs with brown, gray, and purple blotches around the larger end; 2–3 broods per breeding season. The female incubates the eggs; incubation takes 10–12 days. Fledgings leave the nest 7–8 days after hatching.

Food: In summer they eat insects, usually taken from ground. In fall and winter they eat small seeds (grass and weed seeds). They will come to feeders for millet and other small seeds.

Habits: They are persistent singers during the breeding season, and they sing from weed tops, short trees, or other low perches. They do not frequent residential areas.

Fox Sparrow
Passerella iliaca

These large sparrows get
their name from their rusty
upperparts and "foxy-red" tails.
They frequent woodlands and
thickets, especially near water.
They forage on the ground and
usually visit feeders only when
snow covers the ground. Many
people think they are the best
singers in the sparrow family.

Ron Austing

You can attract Fox Sparrows to your backyard by providing water and offering
black oil sunflower seeds, bread crumbs, or millet and other small grains either
on the ground or on platform feeders close to the ground.

Identification Flashes and Distinguishing Features:

Look for large sparrows with gray heads, heavily streaked
underparts, and rufous-red tails.

Size: 7–7½ inches (18–19 centimeters)

Color: They have grayish heads and grayish backs, rufous-red
upperparts and tails, and whitish to pale-gray underparts
with rich rufous streaking that often forms a central stickpin.

Voice: They make clear, flutelike notes that rise and fall in pitch.

Range: They are winter visitors across the Southeast except the
Florida peninsula.

Habitat: They frequent dense woodland thickets and forests. Males
help the females build open-cup nests either on the ground or
close to the ground in small bushes, conifers, or willows.
They make their nests from small twigs, bark strips, grasses,
and weed stems and line them with fine grasses, rootlets,
feathers, and hair (cattle, horse, moose, and caribou).

Eggs: They lay 3–5 pale-green or blue eggs that may have brown
spots; 1 brood per breeding season. The female incubates the
eggs; incubation takes 12–14 days.

Food: They eat primarily seeds, berries, and fruit. They take insects
and other invertebrates on the ground and occasionally forage
on the ground under feeders filled with black oil sunflower
seeds, bread crumbs, or millet or other small grains.

Habits: When foraging on the ground, they dig through leaves,
humus, and snow with a strong towhee-style "double-scratch"
(pushing both feet backward at same time). They often forage
in shadows cast by trees, which camouflages them. They sing
in spring in the Southeast prior to migrating northward. They
are somewhat shy and travel in flocks.

Song Sparrow
Melospiza melodia

Ron Austing

These familiar sparrows nest in hedges and shrubs and forage on the ground beneath feeders. Sometimes called "little brown birds," they are among the least mysterious bird species in North America, thanks to the classic studies of housewife and ornithologist Margaret Morse Nice, who followed the lives of hundreds of individual Song Sparrows around her Ohio home.

You can attract them by including shrubbery in your naturescape, providing water, and offering millet and other small grains on the ground or on platform feeders.

Identification Flashes and Distinguishing Features:

Look for sparrows with heavily streaked underparts and a large central breast spot.

Size: 6¼ inches (16 centimeters)

Color: They have brown upperparts, heavily spotted and streaked whitish underparts, white throats and bellies, gray faces with thin dark lines "through" their eyes, brown malar marks, dark central spot in breasts, thin central crown stripes, and long rounded tails.

Voice: They make quizzical *what?* calls. Their song typically begins with 2-3 clear whistled notes followed by a buzzy trill that sounds like *maids, maids, maids put on your tea kettle-kettle-kettle,* with much variation.

Range: They are permanent residents north of the Cumberlands and Southern Ridge and Valley, Piedmont, and Mid-Atlantic Coastal Plain; they are winter visitors as far south as Tropical Florida.

Habitat: They frequent woodland edges, swamps, roadsides, brushy overgrown fields, hedgerows, cities, and suburbs. Females usually build nests on the ground, well-hidden in the vegetation or close to the ground in low shrubs, thickets, or cattails. They make their nests with grasses, weeds, leaves, and bark and line them with finer grasses, rootlets, and hair.

Eggs: They lay 3–6 pale greenish-white eggs that are almost completely covered with brown, reddish-brown, and gray spots, dots, and blotches; 2–3 broods per breeding season. The female incubates the eggs; incubation takes 12–13 days. Fledglings leave the nest 13–14 days after hatching.

Food: They eat primarily seeds, especially weed seeds, but more than half of their summer diet is insects and other invertebrates (caterpillars, spiders, beetles, ants, wasps, cutworms, army ants, and grasshoppers). They also eat grasses, small fruit, and berries. They forage on the ground under feeders for millet and other small grains.

Habits: They often pump their tails up and down in flight. They sing from elevated perches year-round.

169

Ron Austing

White-throated Sparrow
Zonotrichia albicollis

These plain-breasted, white-throated sparrows have a yellow spot between their eyes and bills. These winter visitors begin singing in late winter or early spring, just before they migrate north.

You can attract White-throated Sparrows to your backyard by including shrubbery and brush piles in your naturescape, providing water, and offering millet and other small grains either on the ground or on platform feeders close to the ground.

Ron Austing

Ron Austing

Identification Flashes and Distinguishing Features:

Look for their dark-and-light striped crowns, yellow lores, and unstreaked breasts.

Size: 6–7 inches (15–18 centimeters)

Color: They have brown upperparts with bold dark to blackish streaking, gray faces and breasts, paler-gray to white bellies and undertail coverts, white throats, white wing bars, and yellow lores. They can have either black heads with white stripes or dark-brown heads with tan to gray stripes.

Voice: They make sharp chink or high-pitched *seeet* notes. They make a thin 2-note whistle followed by 3 sets of triple notes that sounds like *Poor Sam Peabody, Peabody, Peabody.*

Range: They are common winter visitors across the Southeast.

Habitat: They frequent woodland edges, cutover areas, brushy fields, brush piles, and shrubby areas. Females build nesting cups on the ground or in low dense shrubs; their nests are concealed by overhanging vegetation, roots of stump, or rootwad. They make their nests from grass stems, weeds, conifer needles, mosses, bark fibers, and twigs and lined with rootlets, fine grasses, and hair.

Eggs: They lay 3–6 creamy-white, bluish, or greenish eggs that are heavily marked with spots, dots, and blotches of browns, grays, and sometimes black; 1 brood per breeding season. The female incubates the eggs; incubation takes 12–14 days. Fledglings leave the nest 7–12 days after hatching.

Food: They eat primarily small seeds, buds, and a variety of fruit and berries. In spring they may feed on new buds high in trees. They also feed on insects and other invertebrates (crickets, spiders, and beetles). They will come to feeders for black oil sunflower seeds and small grains.

Habits: Flocks live in thickets during the winter. If you make "squeaking" and "pishing" noises on the back of your hand, they (along with chickadees and titmice) will come quickly to investigate.

Ron Austing

White-crowned Sparrow
Zonotrichia leucophrys

They look very similar to White-throated Sparrows but have puffy black-and-white striped crowns and pink bills. They are often found near abandoned farmsteads, feedlots, and hoglots on their wintering grounds in the Southeast.

You can attract White-crowned Sparrows to your backyard by including shrubbery and brush piles in your naturescape, providing water, and offering black oil sunflower seeds, cracked corn, and small grains either on the ground or on platform feeders near the ground.

Ron Austing

Ron Austing

Identification Flashes and Distinguishing Features:

Look for sparrows with unmarked breasts, black-and-white striped crowns, and pink bills.

Size: 7 inches (18 centimeters)

Color: They have brownish upperparts with dark streaking; gray faces, necks, and breasts that blend to buffy wash on their sides and flanks; white throats, bellies, undertail coverts, and wing bars; pink bills; bold black-and-white striped crowns; black lines "through" their eyes; and white lines over their eyes. Juveniles have streaked underparts; immatures look like adults but have tan-and-brown striped heads.

Voice: They sing clear, plaintive *more wet wetter chee zee* whistles.

Range: They are winter visitors as far south as the northern edge of the Mid-Atlantic and East Gulf Coastal Plains.

Habitat: They frequent open country, old brushy fields, and abandoned farmsteads. Females build bulky nesting cups on the ground or close to the ground in shrubs or small trees. They make their nests from weed stems, grasses, mosses, and bark and line them with finer grasses, rootlets, feathers, and hair.

Eggs: They lay 3–5 pale-blue to green eggs heavily spotted with brown, purple, and black; 1 brood per breeding season. The female incubates the eggs; incubation takes 11–16 days. Fledglings leave the nest about 10 days after hatching.

Food: They eat primarily weed seeds, grass seeds, willow catkins, and moss capsules. In summer they feed on insects (ants, mosquitoes, beetles, caterpillars, and spiders). They will come to feeders for black oil sunflower seeds, small grains, and cracked corn.

Habits: When foraging on the ground, they dig through leaves, humus, and snow with a strong towhee-style "double-scratch" (pushing both feet backward at same time). They winter in flocks, often in thickets and brushy areas. They sing in early spring and during migration. If you make "squeaking" and "pishing" noises on the back of your hand, they (along with chickadees and titmice) will come quickly to investigate.

173

Ron Austing

Dark-eyed Junco
Junco hyemalis

Dark-eyed Juncos, a pale-billed subspecies once called Carolina Juncos, visit Southeastern yards, thickets, and old fields during the winter. My grandfather and other country folks always called them "snowbirds."

You can attract Dark-eyed Juncos to your backyard by including shrubbery and brush piles in your naturescape, providing water, and offering black oil sunflower seeds, millet, and other small seeds either on the ground or on platform feeders near the ground.

Ron Austing

Identification Flashes and Distinguishing Features:

Look for their distinctive slate-gray upperparts and white bellies and outer tail feathers (especially seen when they are in flight).

Size: 6¼ inches (16 centimeters)

Color: Males have slate gray heads, upperparts, throats, breasts, sides, and flanks; white bellies, undertail coverts, and outer tail feathers (that flash in flight); and pinkish bone-to-white bills. Females are paler gray, sometimes with a brownish wash.

Voice: They make smacking, sucking *tack, tack, tack* notes and sing one-pitch, jingling, bell-like trills.

Range: They are permanent residents in the hemlock coves, northern hardwoods, and spruce-fir forests of the Southern Blue Ridge area. They are winter visitors across the Southeast except the tip of Tropical Florida.

Habitat: They frequent old brushy-weedy fields, thickets, cedar stands, woodland edges, roadsides, hedges, parks, gardens, and lawns with shrubbery. Females build nesting cups on the ground, often on slopes, banks, edges of trails or roads, and rocky ledges; the nests are concealed by vegetation, rootwads, and fallen logs. Sometimes they build nests in low conifer branches, bushes, or shrubs. They build compact nests from grasses, weed stems, pine needles, mosses, and bark shreds and line them with rootlets, fine grasses, and hair.

Eggs: They lay 3–6 pale bluish-white to gray eggs with heavy spotting and blotches of browns, purples, and grays often concentrated at the larger end; 2 broods per breeding season. The female incubates the eggs; incubation takes 11–13 days. Fledglings leave the nest 12–13 days after hatching.

Food: They eat primarily seeds (grass, weed, and hemlock), fruit, berries, and small grains. Half of their summer diet is insects and other invertebrates. They will come to feeders for black oil sunflower and thistle seeds and "wild bird mix."

Habits: They winter in mixed-species flocks. Aggressive males often spread their tails at rivals, displaying their white outer feathers.

Ron Austing

Red-winged Blackbird
Agelaius phoeniceus

Red-winged Blackbirds can be found along highways, in the willows and cattails bordering fishing holes, and in cultivated fields. They travel and forage with other blackbirds, robins, and starlings, and winter flocks may number into the millions. They migrate northward in early spring, making them the true "harbingers of spring."

You can attract Red-winged Blackbirds to your backyard by providing water and offering millet and other small grains either on the ground or on platform feeders close to the ground.

Ron Austing

Ron Austing

Identification Flashes and Distinguishing Features:

Look for the distinguishing yellow-bordered red shoulder patches on male Red-winged Blackbirds. Females look like large, heavily streaked sparrows and have light lines above their eyes.

Size: 7–9½ inches (18–24 centimeters)

Color: Males have glossy black bodies with red shoulder patches (epaulets) bordered by yellow. Females have brown upperparts, grayish-white underparts heavily streaked with brown, and light lines above their eyes; they may have a red wash on their shoulders, chins, and cheeks.

Voice: Males sing loud, reedy *konk-ah-reee* songs.

Range: They are permanent residents across the Southeast.

Habitat: They frequent freshwater and saltwater marshes, brush and willows bordering water, dry upland fields, wet meadows, and farmlands with tall grasses. Females build loose nesting cups attached by plant fibers to plant stalks or branches. They make their nests from rushes, cattail strips, grasses, rootlets, and mosses and line them with mud and inner linings of finer grasses, hairs, plant down, and rushes.

Eggs: They lay 3–5 pale-blue to green eggs with black, brown, and purple spots, blotches, and scrawls on the larger end; 2 broods per breeding season. The female incubates the eggs; incubation takes 10–12 days. Fledglings leave the nest about 10 days after hatching.

Food: More than 73 percent of their diet is seeds, grains, fruit, and berries. They also eat insects and other invertebrates (beetles, caterpillars, cankerworms, grubs, grasshoppers, spiders, and snails), especially in the summer. They will come to feeders for small mixed seeds, "wildbird mixes," and bread.

Habits: They often live in loose colonies, and males become polygamous if there are surplus females. Males actively defend their territories, driving away predators, other male blackbirds, and cowbirds. Dominant males display red shoulder patches; subordinate males hide them.

Ron Austing

Eastern Meadowlark
Sturnella magna

These are the "field larks" of open grasslands, farmlands, meadows, and pastures. Eastern Meadowlarks spend most of their time on the ground, but singing males prefer high exposed perches on utility wires, fences, and tree-tops. Their white outer tail feathers conspicuously set off their chunky bodies, especially when they are in flight. When flying, they alternately beat their wings swiftly and then glide for brief periods.

You can attract Eastern Meadowlarks to your backyard by offering millet and other small seeds either on the ground or on platform feeders low to the ground in open areas.

Identification Flashes and Distinguishing Features:

Look for the distinguishing bold black "V" on their yellow breasts and conspicuous white outer tail feathers, revealed in flight.

Size: 8¼–10 inches (22–25 centimeters)
Males are larger than females.

Color: They have brownish upperparts streaked with darker browns, blacks, and buff; yellow underparts with bold black "V" on the breast; black streaks and spots on their sides and flanks; and striped buffy-white and blackish-brown heads. Females have narrower breast bands.

Voice: They whisle clear *what, spring is here* slurred notes.

Range: They are permanent residents across the Southeast.

Habitat: They frequent grassy fields, farmlands, pastures, and land bordering airports. Females build nests in grasses on the ground, often shaping nesting cups to fit cow tracks, hoof prints, or other depressions. They make their nests from coarse grasses and line them with finer grasses, pine needles and hair. A grass "dome," with an entrance on one side, conceals the finished nest.

Eggs: They lay 2–7 white eggs liberally spotted with browns, blacks, and lavender on larger ends; 2 broods per breeding season. The female incubates the eggs; incubation takes 13–15 days. Fledglings leave the nest 11–12 days after hatching.

Food: About 75 percent of their diet is insects and other invertebrates (beetles, crickets, grasshoppers, caterpillars, moths, weevils, and cutworms). They also eat weed seeds, grass seeds, and grain.

Habits: They constantly jerk open their tails, revealing their conspicuous white outer tail feathers, as they walk on the ground while foraging. Except for breeding season, they travel in small flocks and family groups.

Ron Austing

179

Boat-tailed Grackle

Quiscalus major

These large blackbirds, with their 7-inch (18 centimeter) keeled tails, stay close to coastal marshes and lowlands. The low-lying terrain of Florida provides the

ideal habitat, and they are common backyard birds across the state. They sing and display noisily from buildings, signs, and utility lines and poles in coastal areas as well as on beaches and dunes.

You can attract them to your backyard by providing water and offering grains either on the ground or on platform feeders low to the ground.

Ron Austing

Identification Flashes and Distinguishing Features:

Look for the large keeled tails on the iridescent blue-purple-black males and bronze-colored females.

Size: Males are 16–17 inches (41–43 centimeters); females are 12–14 inches (30–36 centimeters)

Color: Males have iridescent blue-black bodies with glossy purple upperparts. Females are tawny, buffy brown with darker brown wings and tails.

Voice: They sing a noisy jumble of "electric" whistles, rattles, and loud *jeebs*.

Range: They are permanent residents throughout Florida and in tidal and coastal marshes along the entire East Gulf Coastal Plain, and from Florida through the Carolinas on the Atlantic Coastal Plain, but they are seldom found more than 20 miles inland.

Habitat: They frequent coastal areas, marshes, islands, and land around marinas. Females build nests in bushes and trees near water. They make bulky nesting cups from twigs, reeds, cattails, coarse grasses, paper, string, Spanish moss, rags, cattle dung, or mud and line them with finer grasses, hair, and feathers.

Eggs: They lay 2–5 bluish-gray to pale-blue eggs with brown, black, and lavender dots, blotches, and scrawls; 2 broods per breeding season. The female incubates the eggs; incubation takes 13–14 days. Fledglings leave the nest 20–23 days after hatching.

Food: Primarily eat insects and other invertebrates (grasshoppers, beetles, grubs, snails, mussels, fish, nestlings, eggs, crayfish, shrimps, crabs, frogs, small snakes, and lizards) taken on the ground. Also eat some grains.

Habits: They travel in small flocks except during breeding season, and they nest in loose colonies. They are large, noisy, and conspicuous. Courtship displays of the males include puffing up their plumage, bobbing and bowing to females, and spreading their wings and tails while constantly and loudly vocalizing.

Common Grackle

Quiscalus quiscula

They behave gregariously year-round and winter with other blackbirds, starlings, and robins. Mixed-species flocks can number in the millions.

You can attract Common Grackles to your backyard by providing water and offering millet and other small grains either on the ground or on platform feeders low to the ground.

Ron Austing

Identification Flashes and Distinguishing Features:

You can identify males in flight by their long tails folded into a distinctive keeled-"V" shape.

Size:
11–13½ inches (28–34 centimeters)
Males are larger than females.

Color:
Males have iridescent greenish bodies and heads with a glossy black-purplish sheen; females are duller but blacker. They have long black bills and yellow eyes.

Voice:
They make squeaking sounds that sound like a squeaky gate hinge.

Range;
They are permanent residents across the Southeast.

Habitat:
They frequent a variety of urban and suburban habitats and nest either singly or in small colonies in shrubs, bushes, or deciduous or evergreen trees. Females build loose, bulky nests from weed stalks, grasses, debris, and twigs, sometimes on a mud foundation cup of mud. They line their finished nests with finer grasses, hair, and feathers.

Eggs:
They lay 3–7 pale-greenish to yellow-brown eggs sometimes with brown, black, and lavender spots, blotches, and scrawls concentrated at the larger end; 1 brood per breeding season. The females incubates the eggs; incubation takes 11–14 days. Fledglings leave the nest 14–20 days after hatching.

Food:
They eat a variety of animal fare (tobacco sphinx moths, boll weevils, Japanese beetles, June beetles, wasps, army ants, spiders, earthworms, snails, mice, snakes, lizards, frogs, fish, crayfish, eggs, baby birds, House Sparrows and other small adult birds, and salamanders). They also eat grains, weed seeds, corn, acorns, fruit, and berries.

Habits:
Their gregarious behavior makes them conspicuous along roadways during breeding season. They are often seen in large mixed-species flocks, which invade cities and towns to feed on lawns.

Ron Austing

Brown-headed Cowbird
Molothrus ater

Cowbirds have earned notoriety as brood parasites—they lay their eggs in other birds' nests, leaving the foster parents to raise young cowbirds often at the expense of their own young. Cowbirds may be a factor in the recent population declines of many Southeastern songbirds. Fragmentation of forests and development of open farmlands have benefited this species.

If you want to attract cowbirds, despite their parasitic breeding behavior, place millet and other small grains either on the ground or on platform feeders low to the ground.

Ron Austing

Identification Flashes and Distinguishing Features:

Look for brown-headed birds with a moderately heavy bill.

Size: 7½ inches (19 centimeters)

Color: Males have metallic greenish-black bodies and coffee-brown heads with conical black bills. Females have unmarked ashy brownish-gray coloring. Juveniles are paler than females and have heavily streaked underparts.

Voice: They sing bubbly *glug-glug-glee* notes. The flight note of males is a high-pitched, slurred *cowbird*. Females make dry rattling sounds.

Range: They are permanent residents across the Southeast north of Central Florida. They are winter visitors across the Southeast, including all of Florida.

Habitat: They frequent farmlands, pastures, woodland edges, openings in deciduous and coniferous woodlands, shade trees, and gardens. They do not build nests; they lay their eggs in the nests of at least 214 North American host species.

Eggs: Females usually lay 1 egg each morning and may lay more than 30 eggs per season in host nest(s); some hosts remove cowbird eggs, others build new nests over old ones to cover cowbird eggs, and others abandon their nests. Eggs are white to grayish white with brown speckles concentrated at larger end; incubation takes 11–12 days.

Food: They eat primarily grass seeds, weed seeds, grains, corn, and dandelions. They also eat insects and other invertebrates (grasshoppers, alfalfa weevils, ants, wasps, beetles, spiders, and caterpillars) and some fruit. They will come to feeders for small grains.

Habits: They lift up their tails when they walk. Their genus name, *Molothrus,* means "vagabond." The wandering habits of ancestral cowbirds that followed roaming buffalo herds on the plains may account for their parasitic breeding behavior.

Fred J. Alsop III

Baltimore (Northern) Oriole

Icterus galbula

These showy, musical birds place their distinctive deep-pouch nests so high and so well screened that they're usually not discovered until the leaves fall in autumn, after the birds have already migrated south. They were reclassified in 1973 as Northern Orioles, but new information in 1996 has restored both their name and species status.

You can attract them by providing water, slices of citrus fruit, and feeders filled with suet or commercially available Oriole nectar.

Ron Austing

Identification Flashes and Distinguishing Features:

Look for their orange backs, shoulders, and underparts and black heads, tails, and wings.

Size: 8¾ inches (22 centimeters)

Color: Males have black bodies with bright orange backs, shoulders, underparts, and corner tail patches; females look like washed-out males and have greenish-yellow to yellow-orange bodies and tails. They have dark heads and wings with white wing bars.

Voice: They make clear *hew-it* calls and loud, clear, flutelike songs composed of low-pitched, 2-note phrases broken by softer single notes. They incorporate "chatter" calls into their songs.

Range: They are summer residents across the Southeast north of Florida and the East Gulf and South Atlantic Coastal Plains. They winter in the American tropics.

Habitat: They frequent tall trees in residential areas, streamside borders, roadsides, orchards, and woodland edges. Females weave 5 to 6-inch-deep, grayish pouches suspended by the rim between tree forks or drooping branches. They make their nests from grasses, milkweed fibers, hairs, string (including short strands of yarn), monofilament fishing line, and grapevine bark and line them with finer grasses, hairs, plant fibers, and cottony materials.

Eggs: They lay 4–6 grayish to bluish white eggs with brown and black spots, streaks, and scrawls concentrated at the larger end; 1 brood per breeding season. The female incubates the eggs; incubation takes 12–14 days. Fledglings leave the nest 12–14 days after hatching.

Food: They are especially fond of caterpillars but also eat other insects as well as fruit, berries, and flower nectar. They will come to hummingbird or oriole nectar feeders as well as feeders filled with cut oranges and other citrus fruit, suet, and peanut butter-suet mixes.

Habits: They often nest in yards and sometimes come to feeders. They sing from treetop perches throughout the summer.

House Finch

Carpodacus mexicanus

Ron Austing

In 1940 California cagebird dealers illegally trapped House Finches, a western species, in the wild and shipped them to pet store dealers in New York City for sale as Hollywood Finches or Linnets. The U.S. Fish and Wildlife Service stopped the trafficking, and the New York dealers released their birds into the city. The birds established themselves in the parks and residential areas of the "Big Apple" and have slowly increased their range.

You can attract House Finches by providing water and filling feeders with black oil sunflowers and thistle seeds, "wild bird" mixes, and small grains.

Identification Flashes and Distinguishing Features:

Look for sparrow-size red-and-brown males and streaked brown females.

Size: 6 inches (15 centimeters)

Color: Males have brown upperparts, caps, and ear patches; red rumps, foreheads, eye stripes, chins, throats, and breasts; whitish underparts with brown streaks on their sides and flanks; and whitish wing bars. The amount and intensity of their red coloring varies; some males are orange. Females and juveniles have brown, streaked plumage.

Voice: They make nasal *wheer* calls and high-pitched, warbled 3-note phrases that often end in ascending quizzical notes.

Range: They are permanent residents across the Southeast to the northern East Gulf Coastal Plain and northeastern Florida. They are winter visitors along the Gulf and in northern Florida.

Habitat: They are found in cities, parks, farms, open woods, and suburbs. Females build nests in trees, nesting boxes, ledges, trees, shrubs, ornamental bushes, or vines. They make their nests from grasses, twigs, debris, string, leaves, hair, rootlets, and plant stems and line them with finer materials.

Eggs: They lay 2–6 bluish-white to pale-green eggs speckled with black dots; at least 2 broods per breeding season. The female incubates the eggs; incubation takes 12–16 days. Fledglings leave the nest 11–19 days after hatching.

Food: More than 85 percent of their diet is seeds (grasses, thistle, and dandelion). They also eat some insects. They will come to feeders for thistle and black oil sunflower seeds and small grains.

Habits: They seem to have a commensal relationship with people. Some populations have been stricken with a form of conjunctivitus that produces swollen, crusty eyes and may indirectly cause death in birds that depend on good eyesight for survival. Cleaning feeders regularly and raking away seed hulls and droppings beneath feeders helps control the spread of the disease.

Ron Austing

Purple Finch
Carpodacus purpureus

Superficially similar to the increasingly common House Finches, Purple Finches visit the Southeast only during late fall, winter, and early spring months. They have expanded their breeding range because of the fragmentation of northern coniferous forests, the establishment of Christmas tree farms, and increased plantings of ornamental evergreens and shrubs.

You can easily attract Purple Finches to your backyard by providing water and filling feeders with black oil sunflower seeds.

Ron Austing

Ron Austing

Identification Flashes and Distinguishing Features:

Male Purple Finches look like sparrows that have been dipped in raspberry juice. Look for the broad white stripes above the eyes of the brown females.

Size: 6 inches (15 centimeters)

Color: Males have bright raspberry red heads, backs, rumps, and most of their underparts; whitish lower bellies and undertail coverts; dark lines "through" their eyes; dark wings; and deep forked tails. Females and juveniles have brownish upperparts, gray-brown underparts with heavy brown streaking, wide brown ear patches, and white lines over their eyes.

Voice: They make *chur-lee* calls and rich, rapid, somewhat high-pitched warbles.

Range: They are erratic winter visitors across the Southeast except the Florida peninsula.

Habitat: They frequent open woodlands and suburbs. Females build shallow nesting cups on horizontal branches, usually in conifer trees. They make their nests from twigs, grasses, weed stems, mosses, and rootlets and line them with finer grasses, hair, and wool.

Eggs: They lay 3–6 pale greenish-blue eggs speckled with brown and black; 1 brood per breeding season. The female incubates the eggs; incubation takes 13 days. Fledglings leave the nest about 14 days after hatching.

Food: They eat weeds, grasses, tree seeds, and tree buds. They especially enjoy fruit and berries (blackberry and raspberry). In late spring and summer, they come on insects, particularly caterpillars and beetles. They will come to feeders for black oil sunflower seeds, millet, and small grains.

Habits: They often give their distinctive sharp musical chipping sounds while in flight.

Red Crossbill

Loxia curvirostra

They live in northern coniferous forests but invade the Southeast as far as the Gulf Coastal Plain during years when food is scarce. They usually travel in flocks that bounce through the sky in swift, undulating flight.

You can attract them to your backyard by including pines, hemlocks, and other conifers in your naturescape, providing water, and filling feeders with black oil sunflower seeds.

Fred J. Alsop III

Identification Flashes and Distinguishing Features:

Look for deep-forked tails and crossed mandibles on the brick-red males.

Size: 5½–6½ inches (14–17 centimeters)

Color: Males have brick-red upperparts, with the brightest red on their rumps, and blackish wings and tails. Females are dull yellow overall with dark-brown to black wings and tails. Adults have crossed bills; recently fledged juveniles have uncrossed bills. Juveniles look like females but with streaked underparts.

Voice: They give distinctive *jip, jip, jip* calls in flight. They also sing whistled and warbled phrases.

Range: They are uncommon permanent residents in the Southern Blue Ridge mountains in Tennessee and North Carolina. During severe northern winters, they are irruptive visitors across the Southeast and into the Deep South.

Habitat: They live in northern coniferous forests, and females conceal their nests in the needles of horizontal conifer branches. They build loosely-constructed nesting cups from twigs, rootlets, bark strips, and lichens; they line their finished nests with finer grasses, mosses, hair, and feathers.

Eggs: They lay 3–5 pale-blue to greenish eggs spotted with browns and black; 1 brood per breeding season. The female incubates the eggs; incubation takes 12–14 days. Fledglings leave the nest about 17 days after hatching, with their bills still uncrossed.

Food: They feed on seeds of deciduous trees. They also take insects (ants, caterpillars, beetles, and aphids). They are fond of calcium salts and during winter often flock to mortar joints or sides of roads that have been salted for ice removal. They will come to feeders for sunflower and other seeds.

Habits: When foraging, they appear to be little twittering parrots as they scramble over branches using their feet and crossed bills. They use their highly adapted crossed bills and tongues to extract seeds from conifer cones. They nest almost any month of the year depending on food abundance and sometimes linger to nest south of normal breeding range during invasion years. They are often tame and easily approachable.

Pine Siskin
Carduelis pinus

Fred J. Alsop III

These small brownish, heavily streaked northern finches reach the Gulf Coast and Florida during winter invasions. When their boreal forest evergreen seed supply is sparse, irruptive flocks may turn up in conifers or at feeders across the Southeast.

You can attract Pine Siskins to your backyard by providing water and filling feeders with thistle or black oil sunflower seeds.

Identification Flashes and Distinguishing Features:

Look for brown, heavily streaked sparrow-size birds that have small bills and yellow streaks in their wings and tails.

Size: 5 inches (13 centimeters)

Color: They have gray-brown upperparts and buffy-white underparts with heavy streaking above and below; buffy-white wing bars; broad yellow stripes that show as yellow patches on folded wings; and dark, short notched tails with some yellow plumage.

Voice: They make notes that resemble a miniature chain saw and American Goldfinch-like songs with buzzy *shreeeeeee* notes.

Range: They are erratic winter visitors across the Southeast except peninsular Florida. They occasionally breed in the high elevation spruce-fir forests of the Southern Blue Ridge mountains in eastern Tennessee and western North Carolina.

Habitat: They frequent coniferous forests as well as evergreens in parks, cemeteries, suburbs, and gardens. Females build nests on horizontal conifer branches; the nests are well-concealed by needles. They make shallow nesting cups from twigs, needles, grasses, bark, mosses, and lichens and line them with finer grasses, mosses, rootlets, hair, fur, and feathers.

Eggs: They lay 2–6 pale bluish to greenish eggs with black, brown, and lavender dots and spots concentrated at the larger end, often forming a wreath; 1–2 broods per breeding season. The female incubates the eggs, and the male feeds her while she is on the nest; incubation takes 13 days. Fledglings leave the nest about 15 days after hatching.

Food: They feed on seeds of conifer and deciduous trees as well as weed and grass seeds and thistle. In late spring and summer they take insects (aphids, beetles, and caterpillars) and also drink sap from sapsucker drill wells. They are fond of calcium salts and during winter often flock to mortar joints or sides of roads that have been salted for ice removal. They will come to feeders for thistle, black oil sunflower, and other small seeds.

Habits: They are extremely tame and approachable and sometimes will eat from your hand. They enjoy bathing and drinking at birdbaths.

Fred J. Alsop III

American Goldfinch
Carduelis tristis

My grandfather and many other country people call these bright yellow-and-black birds "Wild Canaries." The genus name *Carduelis* refers to their fondness for thistle. The species name tristis means "sad" and points to their often heard plaintive *dear-me! (babeee)* notes.

You can attract American Goldfinches to your backyard by including late summer and early fall wildflowers in your naturescape, providing water, and filling feeders with black oil sunflower seeds or thistle.

Ron Austing

Ron Austing

Identification Flashes and Distinguishing Features:

In spring look for the unmistakable bright "canary" yellow and black cap, wings, and tails of male American Goldfinches.

Size: 5 inches (13 centimeters)

Color: In spring males have bright yellow bodies, white rumps and undertail coverts, and black caps, notched tails, and wings with white bars. Females are duller yellow overall with olive-green backs and no black caps. During winter both males and females are browner and greener overall; males do not have black caps and may show more yellow wash than females.

Voice: They make distinctive *per-CHICK-o-ree* calls when in flight. They also sing canary-like series of twitters, chips, and trills with *swee* or *babeee* notes incorporated into songs.

Range: They are permanent residents across the Southeast north of the East Gulf and Mid-Atlantic Coastal Plains and Florida. They are winter visitors across the entire Southeast.

Habitat: They frequent areas abundant in thistle, including open country, overgrown fields, vacant lots, towns, suburbs, and other areas with scattered trees. Females build well-woven nesting cups in weed patches, brier patches, shrubs, vines, and trees. They make their nests from plant fibers and line them with milkweed, thistle, or cattail down.

Eggs: They lay 4–6 unmarked pale bluish-white eggs; 1 brood per breeding season. The female incubates the eggs, and the male feeds her when she is on the nest; incubation takes 12–14 days. Fledglings leave the nest 10–16 days after hatching.

Food: They prefer thistle seeds but also eat weed, grass, and tree seeds and catkins, tree buds, and flower heads. They also take insects, some fruit, and berries. They will come to feeders for thistle, small grains, and black oil sunflower seeds.

Habits: They nest in late summer when small seeds from wildflowers and weeds are readily available; adults feed regurgitated seeds to their young. They remain in flocks until July, when they pair for breeding.

Evening Grosbeak
Coccothraustes vespertinus

At first glance you might mistake these northern finches for large goldfinches until you notice the massive white bills and dark heads of the males. These birds are something special. Evening Grosbeaks live in northern coniferous forests, but every third or fourth winter when their populations are large or the supply of tree seeds is small, they invade the South, sometimes in huge numbers.

You can attract Evening Grosbeaks to your backyard by providing water and filling feeders with black oil sunflower seeds.

Ron Austing

Identification Flashes and Distinguishing Features:

Look for large yellow, black, and white males and gray and white females with big bills. Listen for their loud, strident calls.

Size: 8 inches (20 centimeters)

Color: Males have burnt to bright-yellow bodies; black wings with large white patches; black notched tails; blackish heads, throats, and breasts; yellow foreheads, lores, and stripes over eyes; and massive white (pale greenish in the spring) bills. Females and juveniles have silver-gray upperparts, buffy underparts, black wings and tails with white patches, white throats, yellowish collars, and large white bills.

Voice: They make loud, far-carrying House Sparrow-like *peet peet kreeck* calls and Purple Finch-like songs.

Range: These erratic wintering northern finches can be found as far south as the northern reaches of the East Gulf and Mid-Atlantic Coastal Plains.

Habitat: They frequent coniferous forests. Females weave shallow nests on conifer branches hidden by needles and sometimes in deciduous trees or shrubs. Their nesting cups are interwoven twigs, mosses, and lichen, lined with rootlets.

Eggs: They lay 2–5 bluish-green eggs with brown, gray, purple, and black spots and specklings; 1 brood per breeding season. The female incubates the eggs; incubation takes 12–14 days. Fledglings leave the nest 13–14 days after hatching.

Food: They eat primarily tree seeds and buds. In summer they take insects (cankerworms, spruce budworms, and beetles). They also eat fruit and berries (dogwood, cherries, and choke-cherries). They will come to feeders for sunflower seeds.

Habits: They make themselves welcome at backyard feeders when they invade the Southeast. They travel in flocks most of the year. They are fond of calcium salts and during winter often flock to mortar joints or sides of roads that have been salted for ice removal; unfortunately many are killed by vehicles. They drink water from birdbaths.

House Sparrow
Passer domesticus

Ron Austing

The species name *domesticus* means "about the house," which describes this bird's surroundings—they live where people live. Introduced into New York City in the nineteenth century, this European species has spread across North America.

You can attract House Sparrows by providing water and nesting boxes with holes at least 1½ inches in diameter. Placing a dowel perch beneath the hole will encourage them to nest in the box. You can also attract them by offering millet, "wild bird mixes," and other small seeds.

Identification Flashes and Distinguishing Features:

Look for the gray crowns and black bibs and chins on males. Look for the yellowish bills and tan eye stripes on females.

Size: 6¼ inches (16 centimeters)

Color: Males have rich brown upperparts streaked with black; ashy-buff underparts; gray crowns, cheeks, and rumps; white wing bars and face patches; black lores, chins, and bibs; and blackish conical beaks. Females have brown upperparts with blackish streaks, ashy-buff underparts with indistinct streaking, buffy lines over their eyes, and yellowish bills.

Voice: They make loud, repeated *cheap, cheap, cheap* sounds.

Range: They are permanent residents across the Southeast.

Habitat: They can be found in cities, suburbs, parks, farms, and along highways. Both parents build a nest in natural cavities, nesting boxes, holes in buildings, behind shutters, on rafters, under eaves, and behind highway signs. They make their nests from grasses, debris, string, paper, weeds, and straw and line them with feathers. A bulky dome conceals the finished nest.

Eggs: They lay 3–7 whitish, blue-white, or green-white eggs with tan, brown, and gray spots and blotches; 2–3 broods per breeding season. The female incubates the eggs; incubation takes 11–14 days. Fledglings leave the nest 13–17 days after hatching.

Food: In spring and summer they feed on insects and other invertebrates (ants, worms, crickets, grasshoppers, beetles, wasps, moths, flies, caterpillars, and spiders). They also take fruit, seeds, and waste grains (corn, oats, and wheat). They will come to feeders for millet, wheat, and other small grains.

Habits: They are usually seen in noisy flocks and sleep in communal roosts, except during breeding season, in shrubs, conifers, or ivy vines on the sides of buildings. House Sparrows used to have commensal relationships with horses and picked undigested grain seeds from their droppings. When horse populations began to decline around the turn of the century with the coming of the automobile, House Sparrow populations declined as well.

Helpful Resource Materials

Books

Adler, Bill Jr. *Outwitting Squirrels: 101 Cunning Stratagems to Reduce Dramatically the Egregious Misappropriation of Seed from Your Birdfeeder by Squirrels.* Chicago: Chicago Review Press, 1996.

Bierly, Michael Lee. *Bird Finding in Tennessee.* MIchael Lee Bierly, 1980.

Bio-Intergral Resource Center. *Common Sense Pest Control Quarterly.* Berkeley: B.I.R.C.

Buff, Sheila. *The Birdfeeder's Handbook.* New York: Lyons & Burford Pub., 1991.

Burton, Robert. *The National Audubon Society North American Birdfeeder Handbook.* New York: Dorling Kindersley Publishing Inc., 1995.

Clench, Mary H. and Sally H. Spofford. *Attracting Birds to Your Back Yard.* 1991.

Dennis, John V. *A Complete Guide to Birdfeeding.* New York: Alfred A. Knopf, 1975.

Dennis, John V. *The Wildlife Gardener.* New York: Alfred A. Knopf Inc., 1985.

Dennis, John V., Michael McKinley, and editorial staff at Ortho Books. *How to Attract Birds.* Ortho Information Services, 1983.

Harrison, George H. *Backyard Bird Watcher.* New York: Simon and Schuster, 1979.

Henderson, Carrol L. *Landscaping for Wildlife.* St. Paul: Minnesota Dept. of Natural Resources, 1987.

——————. *Wild About Birds: The DNR Birdfeeding Guide.* Minn: Minnesota's Bookstore, 1995.

Imhof, Thomas A. *Alabama Birds,* 2nd ed. University of Alabama: University of Alabama Press, 1976.

Jones, John Oliver. *Where the Birds Are: A Guide to All 50 States and Canada.* New York: William Morrow and Col Inc., 1990.

Kress, Stephen W. *The Audubon Society Guide to Attracting Birds.* New York: Simon and Schuster, 1979.

——————. *The National Audubon Society Bird Garden.* New York: Dorling Kindersley Publishing, 1995.

Lowery, George H., Jr. *Louisiana Birds,* 3rd ed. Baton Rouge: Louisiana State University Press, 1974.

Merilees, William J. *Attracting Backyard Wildlife.* Still Water: Voyageur Press Inc., 1989.

Mohrhardt, David and Richard E. Schinkel. *Suburban Nature Guide.* Harrisburg: Stackpole Books, 1991.

National Geographic Society. *Field Guide to the Birds of North America*, 2nd ed. Washington, D.C.: National Geographic Society, 1987.

National Wildlife Federation. *Gardening With Wildlife Kit*. Washington, D.C.: National Wildlife Federation, 1990.

Pettingill, Olin Sewall, Jr. *A Guide to Bird Finding East of the Mississippi*, 2nd ed. New York: Oxford University Press, 1977.

Porter, Eloise F., James F. Parnell, and Robert P. Teulings. *Birds of the Carolinas*. Chapel Hill: The Univeristy of North Carolina Press, 1980.

Schultz, Warren. *The Chemical-Free Lawn*. Emmaus: Rodale Press, 1989.

Smyser, Carol A. and Rodale Press Editors. *Nature's Design*. Emmaus: Rodale Press, 1982.

Stokes, Donald. *The Bird Feeder Book*. Canada: Little, Brown & Company, 1987.

Stokes, Donald and Lillian Stokes. *The Hummingbird Book*. Boston: Little, Brown & Company, 1989.

Tekulsky, Mathew. *The Butterfly Garden*. Boston: The Harvard Common Press, 1985.

—————. *The Hummingbird Garden*. New York: Crown Publishing Group, 1990.

Terres, John K. *Songbirds in Your Garden*. Algonquin Books of Chapel Hill, 1994.

Tufts, Craig E. *The Backyard Naturalist*. Washington, D.C.: National Wildlife Federation, 1987.

U.S. Fish and Wildlife Service, *Okefenokee National Wildlife Refuge*. Greer Consulting Services Inc., 1997.

Witty, Dick and Helen Witty. *Feed the Birds*. New York: Workman Publishing, 1991.

Xerces Society. *Butterfly Gardening*. San Francisco: Sierra Club Books, 1990.

Videotapes

Attracting Birds to Your Backyard with Roger Tory Peterson, produced by Nature Science Network.

Birds of the Backyard: Winter into Spring with George Harrison, produced by Company for Home Entertainment.

How to Start Birdwatching with Diane Porter, 1994.

Hummingbirds Up Close, produced by Nature Science Network,1988.

Audiotapes

Backyard Bird Songs, produced by Houghton Mifflin as part of the Peterson Field Guide Series, 1991.

Index

American Crow, 124
American Goldfinch, 190
American Kestrel
  (Sparrow Hawk), 94
American Robin, 144
Baltimore (Northern) Oriole,
  184
Barn Swallow, 120
Blackbird, Red-winged,
  176
Blue Jay, 122
Blue-gray Gnatcatcher, 140
Bluebird, Eastern, 141
Boat-tailed Grackle, 180
Bobwhite, Northern, 95
Brown Creeper, 133
Brown Thrasher, 146
Brown-headed Cowbird,
  182
Brown-headed Nuthatch,
  132
Bunting(s)
  Indigo, 160
  Painted, 162
Cardinal, Northern, 157
Carolina Chickadee, 126
Carolina Wren, 134
Catbird, Gray, 145
Cedar Waxwing, 148
Chickadee, Carolina, 126
Chipping Sparrow, 165
Common Grackle, 181
Common Ground-Dove, 101
Common Nighthawk, 102
Cooper's Hawk, 92
Cowbird, Brown-headed,
  182
Creeper, Brown, 133
Crossbill, Red, 188
Crow(s)
  American, 124
  Fish, 125
Dark-eyed Junco, 174
Dove(s)
  Common Ground-, 101
  Eurasian Collared, 100
  Mourning, 99
  Rock (Pigeon), 97
  White-winged, 98

Downy Woodpecker, 112
Eastern Bluebird, 141
Eastern Meadowlark, 178
Eastern Phoebe, 117
Eastern Screech-Owl, 103
Eastern (Rufous-sided)
  Towhee, 164
Eurasian Collared Dove, 100
European Starling, 149
Evening Grosbeak, 192
Field Sparrow, 166
Finch(es)
  House, 185
  Purple, 186
Fish Crow, 125
Flicker, Northern
  (Yellow-shafted), 115
Flycatcher, Great Crested,
  118
Fox Sparrow, 168
Gnatcatcher, Blue-gray, 140
Golden-crowned Kinglet,
  138
Goldfinch
  American, 190
Grackle(s)
  Boat-tailed, 180
  Common, 181
Gray Catbird, 145
Great Crested Flycatcher,
  118
Grosbeak(s)
  Evening, 192
  Rose-breasted, 158
Hairy Woodpecker, 114
Hawk(s)
  Cooper's, 92
  Sharp-shinned, 91
  Sparrow (see Kestrel,
    American)
Hermit Thrush, 142
House Finch, 185
House Sparrow, 193
House Wren, 136
Hummingbird(s)
  Ruby-throated, 104
  Rufous, 106
Indigo Bunting, 160
Jay, Blue, 122

Junco, Dark-eyed, 174
Kestrel, American
   (Sparrow Hawk), 94
Killdeer, 96
Kinglet(s)
   Golden-crowned, 138
   Ruby-crowned, 139
Martin, Purple, 119
Meadowlark, Eastern, 178
Mockingbird, Northern,
   147
Mourning Dove, 99
Nighthawk, Common, 102
Northern Bobwhite, 95
Northern Cardinal, 157
Northern (Yellow-shafed)
   Flicker, 115
Northern Mockingbird, 147
Nuthatch(es)
   Brown-headed, 132
   Red-breasted, 130
   White-breasted, 131
Oriole, Baltimore (Northern),
   184
Owl, Eastern Screech-, 103
Painted Bunting, 162
Palm Warbler, 154
Phoebe, Eastern, 117
Pigeon (see Rock Dove)
Pileated Woodpecker, 116
Pine Siskin, 189
Pine Warbler, 152
Purple Finch, 186
Purple Martin, 119
Red Crossbill, 188
Red-bellied Woodpecker,
   108
Red-breasted Nuthatch, 130
Red-eyed Vireo, 150
Red-headed Woodpecker,
   107
Red-winged Blackbird, 176
Robin, American, 144
Rock Dove (Pigeon), 97
Rose-breasted Grosbeak,
   158
Ruby-crowned Kinglet, 139
Ruby-throated
   Hummingbird, 104
Rufous Hummingbird, 106
Sapsucker, Yellow-bellied,
   110
Sharp-shinned Hawk, 91

Siskin, Pine, 189
Song Sparrow, 169
Sparrow(s)
   Chipping, 165
   Field, 166
   Fox, 168
   House, 193
   Song, 169
   White-crowned, 172
   White-throated, 170
Starling, European, 149
Swallow(s)
   Barn, 120
   Tree, 121
Thrasher, Brown, 146
Thrush(es)
   Hermit, 142
   Wood, 143
Titmouse, Tufted, 128
Towhee, Eastern (Rufous-
   sided), 164
Tree Swallow, 121
Tufted Titmouse, 128
Vireo, Red-eyed, 150
Warbler(s)
   Palm, 154
   Pine, 152
   Yellow-rumped (Myrtle),
      151
   Yellow-throated, 156
Waxwing, Cedar, 148
White-breasted Nuthatch,
   131
White-crowned Sparrow,
   172
White-throated Sparrow,
   170
White-winged Dove, 98
Wood Thrush, 143
Woodpecker(s)
   Downy, 112
   Hairy, 114
   Pileated, 116
   Red-bellied, 108
   Red-headed, 107
Wren(s)
   Carolina, 134
   House, 136
Yellow-bellied Sapsucker,
   110
Yellow-rumped (Myrtle)
   Warbler, 151
Yellow-throated Warbler, 156

About the Author

Fred J. Alsop III holds a Ph.D. degree in zoology from the University of Tennessee at Knoxville and teaches biological sciences at East Tennessee State University. A Kentucky native, Fred is an avid birder and field biologist who has identified more than 2,600 species of birds in eighteen countries and has lead natural history tours to many parts of the world. He has photographed birds for more than twenty-five years, and his photographs have appeared in numerous calendars, books, and magazines.

Fred has published more than 125 articles and notes on birds in state, regional, national, and international journals. He is the author of Birds of the Smokies, a national award-winning book, and coauthor with Dr. David H. Snyder of Birds of Land Between the Lakes.

He has served two terms as a national lecturer for the Research Society of Sigma Xi and has taught numerous workshops for state and federal wildlife officers and biologists on field identification of birds as part of the international Partners in Flight program. He is recognized as an authority on the avifauna of Tennessee.

Fred is a public speaker, scuba diver, private pilot, and tennis player. He and his wife, Cathi, live in Johnson City, Tennessee.

Birdwatching Checklist

Use the **Which is it?** checklist to help you identify birds.

Where and When	**Identification flashes**
Habitat	**Sounds**
Impression	
Comparison	**Important details**
Habits	**Tail and wings**

___ American Crow (page 124)
___ American Goldfinch (page 190)
___ American Kestrel (Sparrow Hawk; page 94)
___ American Robin (page 144)
___ Baltimore (Northern) Oriole (page 184)
___ Barn Swallow (page 120)
___ Blue Jay (page 122)
___ Blue-gray Gnatcatcher (page 140)
___ Boat-tailed Grackle (page 180)
___ Brown Creeper (page 133)
___ Brown Thrasher (page 146)
___ Brown-headed Cowbird (page 182)
___ Brown-headed Nuthatch (page 132)
___ Carolina Chickadee (page 126)
___ Carolina Wren (page 134)
___ Cedar Waxwing (page 148)
___ Chipping Sparrow (page 165)
___ Common Grackle (page 181)
___ Common Ground-Dove (page 101)
___ Common Nighthawk (page 102)
___ Cooper's Hawk (page 92)
___ Dark-eyed Junco (page 174)
___ Downy Woodpecker (page 112)
___ Eastern Bluebird (page 141)
___ Eastern Meadowlark (page 178)
___ Eastern Phoebe (page 117)
___ Eastern (Rufous-sided) Towhee (page 164)
___ Eastern Screech-Owl (page 103)
___ Eurasian Collared Dove (page 100)
___ European Starling (page 149)
___ Evening Grosbeak (page 192)
___ Field Sparrow (page 166)
___ Fish Crow (page 125)
___ Fox Sparrow (page 168)
___ Golden-crowned Kinglet (page 138)

___ Gray Catbird (page 145)
___ Great Crested Flycatcher (page 118)
___ Hairy Woodpecker (page 114)
___ Hermit Thrush (page 142)
___ House Finch (page 185)
___ House Sparrow (page 193)
___ House Wren (page 136)
___ Indigo Bunting (page 160)
___ Killdeer (page 96)
___ Mourning Dove (page 99)
___ Northern Bobwhite (page 95)
___ Northern Cardinal (page 157)
___ Northern (Yellow-shafted) Flicker (page 115)
___ Northern Mockingbird (page 147)
___ Painted Bunting (page 162)
___ Palm Warbler (page 154)
___ Pileated Woodpecker (page 116)
___ Pine Siskin (page 189)
___ Pine Warbler (page 152)
___ Purple Finch (page 186)
___ Purple Martin (page 119)
___ Red Crossbill (page 188)
___ Red-bellied Woodpecker (page 108)
___ Red-breasted Nuthatch (page 130)
___ Red-eyed Vireo (page 150)
___ Red-headed Woodpecker (page 107)
___ Red-winged Backbird (page 176)
___ Rock Dove (Pigeon; page 97)
___ Rose-breasted Grosbeak (page 158)
___ Ruby-crowned Kinglet (page 139)
___ Ruby-throated Hummingbird (page 104)
___ Rufous Hummingbird (page 106)
___ Sharp-shinned Hawk (page 91)
___ Song Sparrow (page 169)
___ Tree Swallow (page 121)
___ Tufted Titmouse (page 128)
___ White-breasted Nuthatch (page 131)
___ White-crowned Sparrow (page 172)
___ White-throated Sparrow (page 170)
___ White-winged Dove (page 98)
___ Wood Thrush (page 143)
___ Yellow-bellied Sapsucker (page 110)
___ Yellow-rumped (Myrtle) Warbler (page 151)
___ Yellow-throated Warbler (page 156)